The Kid in

Purple Pants

Structured Approaches to
Educating Underprivileged Students

Patrick Anderson

First printing,
November, 2012

►Cover Design by Brad Keim
►Proofreading by Marcia Abramson

ISBN 978-0-982663561

Also available in eBook format: ISBN 978-0-982663578

The Kid in Purple Pants

Structured Approaches to Educating Underprivileged Students

2

Table of Contents

The Kid in Purple Pants

Structured Approaches to Educating Underprivileged Students

Dedication

To Kim, Taylor, and Scotty

Special thanks to

Brad Keim, Cover Artist
Keri O'Brien, Editing

Legal Disclaimer

The ideas, suggestions, and advice provided in this book are those of the authors. While every effort has been made to present sound and accurate legal and practical guidance, the information herein is not warranted and does not constitute legal advice. The reader should be aware that the field of education law is in a constant state of change. Additionally, the facts in specific situations and the laws of certain jurisdictions may change the recommendations and suggestions rendered herein. Readers are strongly encouraged to check with private legal counsel before undertaking any decision that may require legal guidance or implementing or adopting any policy, procedure, or practice.

The Kid in Purple Pants

Structured Approaches to Educating Underprivileged Students

Introduction

"Having been poor is no shame,
but being ashamed of it, is."

—Benjamin Franklin

When I started writing this book I asked myself: Why are you writing about your childhood? Why are you powerless to stop bringing up all that insane stuff that happened to you in fifth grade? Why do you tell others you wore purple pants?

How did it even fit on these pages? Who really cared? It seemed misplaced, a mishmash, too personal when my real purpose was to create a book that outlines the best practices for teaching economically disadvantaged students—poor kids. Why insist on parading my past for all to read?

It was only after I finished the manuscript and rewrote it that it all made sense.

What I felt and knew as a kid made me the person to advocate for all the students who are now growing up exactly like I did—poor, confused, scared, and trying to hide their feelings of insecurity.

I hope you enjoy the glimpses of my life as they appear in these pages. My experiences are what drive me now to be more conscious of what I do and say every single day that I walk into a school building. They are why I am suggesting a different approach to educating students who come from poor or poverty-stricken homes. And it's why I focus on myself and what I saw and felt.

The Kid in Purple Pants

Structured Approaches to Educating Underprivileged Students

5

After that pivotal fifth grade, I've been an educator for 20 great years, as a teacher, principal, and now superintendent. From every level I've seen too many kids like me lost in the system, and the system and America poorer for their exclusion. That has to change if we want to meet the needs of *all* our children while simultaneously and systematically improving our ability to fully educate.

Fortunately, I'm not alone. Ruby Payne, Jonathan Kozol, and a host of others have long been writing about poverty and the needs of our poor children as they relate to education. I deeply respect them, and their knowledge has been extremely influential on my approach to teaching and administration. I know that I'm not in the same league with Payne or Kozol. I am simply the son of a roofer dad and a waitress mom. I'm a little brother, a big brother, a father, a husband, and an educator who has witnessed what it takes to meet the needs of students who require more guidance and support if they are to be successful in an education system designed now to induce them to fail.

I also was the only kid in my school who wore purple pants. If you were poor, you wore the only pants you had. So I am sharing what I know firsthand, true stories of what life was like as a poor student struggling to overcome his own insecurities about what he could ultimately become. I hope it helps provide educators and administrators with ideas of how organizational changes in the daily practice of education can bring about a real transformation for underprivileged students.

The Kid in Purple Pants

Structured Approaches to Educating Underprivileged Students

Chapter 1

The Kid in Purple Pants

"Poverty of goods is easily cured;
poverty of the mind is irreparable."

—Michel Eyquem de Montaigne

I was a poor kid. Don't get me wrong; I wasn't a child living in poverty. Specifically, I wasn't categorized as rich, middle class, or lower middle class. My family was just poor. My parents kept my siblings and me fed, happy, well-adjusted, and very much loved. Yet we also lived beyond our economic means. We bounced and floated bad checks, enjoyed dinners we shouldn't have eaten, and took mini-vacations and trips we shouldn't have, which in many ways made it feel as though we weren't poor, even though we really were. It wasn't until I was grown that I understood why we lived so far beyond our means. It was my parents' way of providing their children a little social equity. It was what gave them the desire to pack five kids into a rented passenger van and take them from southern Illinois to Biloxi, Mississippi, to see the Gulf of Mexico for the first time when they could no more afford to do it than buy the Gateway Arch in St. Louis.

So it's no wonder that, until one fall day in the fifth grade, I had no idea I was poor and a little different than most of my friends. Until that memorable day, I was just another kid, attending school, playing with my siblings and friends, learning, and enjoying everything—including school.

The Kid in Purple Pants

Structured Approaches to Educating Underprivileged Students

A Perfect Beginning

I remember my utter joy about starting kindergarten. I was elated to finally attend school. I began my education at Lewis and Clark Elementary, a small public school in southern Illinois that was situated cattycorner from St. Bernard's, the Catholic school my older brothers attended. I was going to Lewis and Clark because St. Bernard's did not yet offer kindergarten in 1976. It didn't matter to me that I wasn't at the same school as my brothers because Vince and Misty were going to kindergarten too. They were even assigned to Mrs. Barnard's afternoon class with me.

Vince and Misty were the twins who lived five houses down the alley from my family. We were best friends from the neighborhood and had spent the first five years of our lives walking up and down the alley and playing in each other's backyards.

Before I had even stepped into the classroom, my brothers had already told me all about kindergarten. It was fun, they said, and you didn't have to do much work. You played all the time, got free graham crackers and milk, and you only had to go for half a day. It was the best year of your life, they said. And they were right!

I loved walking through the doors of the school knowing I would see Vince and Misty in that amazing building and fun-filled classroom. We had everything we could ever imagine in that kindergarten class. Little cardboard boxes that looked like bricks were among my favorite toys. We would stack them to build walls that we would then knock down. An entire cardboard box full of old faucets; pieces of long, threaded steel pipe, and oversized bolts and nuts was located in the back of the endless play area. And any hat a five-year-old ever wanted

The Kid in Purple Pants

Structured Approaches to Educating Underprivileged Students

8

to wear was available to pretend to be a fireman, police officer, or Indian chief. To me, it was paradise.

At the risk of repeating a cliché, I really did learn everything I needed to know in kindergarten. I concentrated and focused harder on those cardboard-brick buildings and faucet-handled "swords" more than I have ever focused on anything since. I was given an opportunity to learn and explore on my own. I had no script to follow and learned from investigating my surroundings, collaborating with friends, and trial and error. I learned the benefits of cooperation, how to respect the opinions of others, compassion, and the joys of friendship. Heaven. I wasn't afforded those same opportunities while studying John Milton my senior year in college, where the students only looked after themselves.

First grade was much the same experience; even better, I could go to school for the whole day. I remember learning to read that year and some of my very first spelling tests, which I cherished. Spelling was my favorite subject because I was good at it. We had our tests on Fridays. On Thursday nights my Mom would sit down with me and teach me that week's words. I loved how she would get so excited when I spelled a word correctly and how she would scold my brothers when they teased me for having difficulty with one of the words. The test I remember most dealt with homophones. My Mom had warned me to not be tricked when the teacher read the sentences and that we would have to spell the correct word based on the sentence and how the word was being used. She stressed and stressed that the "meet" that you use when you get a new friend had two e's and the "meat" you eat had "eat" in it. She was a genius.

I took the homophone test almost 35 years ago, yet I remember it more than any other test I have taken since. I sat on my feet and knees, and I remember pushing my haunches

The Kid in Purple Pants

Structured Approaches to Educating Underprivileged Students

against the back of the chair through the entire test, smiling as I completed the work. Miss Magurany, as I recall, was just as excited about the test as I was. I focused hard on each syllable coming out of her mouth and knew there was no way I was going to be fooled. And I was right. The teacher was practically giving us the answers! She spoke in such sentences as "Meet. Pat and Katie will meet new friends on the field trip. Meet." My mind was thinking: Oh my god, how easy was this lady going to make this test? I could never fail. I earned a 100% on that test and raced straight home to tell my Mom of my success in conquering the task put before me. I showed her my reward, which was a huge sticker of a brown bear swinging a baseball bat.

I began learning how to write cursive in second grade. Looking back, I have no clue as to why it was imperative to learn cursive writing at such a young age, but I admit that I loved the challenge. I had a bunch of big loops in my name and I took pleasure in trying to make them look exactly like they did on the chalkboard. Miss Patrick loved the way I made my P's and said she thought my A's were perfect. I learned the joys of doing more than what was expected of me and that hard work pays dividends.

Social studies and the seven continents are what I remember most about my education in third grade. Well, almost. What I remember *most* was that we had the "hottest" teacher in the entire world for third grade, according to the older students. I remember them teasing us about having a hot teacher and my brothers telling us we were "so stupid" because we just didn't get how much of a "fox" she was. Spelling words got harder, but we had a huge chart where our teacher would place stars when we earned a 100% on tests. The girls scored better than the boys, but we still got our fair share of stars.

The Kid in Purple Pants

Structured Approaches to Educating Underprivileged Students

I loved the relationships I was starting to build. I had brothers and a sister, but this was different. These kids were people I "chose" to be friends with, and who chose to befriend me. As far back as third grade we started opening up to one another and even talked about "Hotsy Totsy" (our teacher, Mrs. Totzell). I loved the laughter we shared and the inside jokes we would tell. And the icing on the cake: I could run faster than any boy in my class.

I know I must have learned a few things in fourth grade, but I honestly don't remember much about that year. I recall that my older brothers were again dead-on about what to expect. They said fourth grade was a little boring and you did a horde of worksheets and tons of fraction and decimal problems, and that math was a big deal. How could two boys who cussed and fought (and were so not the little altar boys they played in school) be so right about everything? I still don't understand it. In my year of being a fourth-grader, I was "drilled and killed" on how to simplify, multiply, and divide fractions and how to add, subtract, and convert fractions into decimals. The work wasn't as much "fun," but it was still a challenge I enjoyed. Mrs. Kravenak never stopped telling us how "proud" she was to have us in her class.

One of my favorite days of fourth grade was when my Dad came to school to talk about what he did for a living. I was beyond excited about it, and my Dad put the date in his calendar so he wouldn't forget. At the time, he was selling real estate for Century 21. I don't think he was doing much selling, however, because interest rates were hovering around 12%. To help make ends meet, my father had also started a construction company and was trying to get it off the ground. During his visit to my school, he wore the Century 21 gold jacket and a nametag that, to a fourth-grader, made him look more important than the president. He came and talked to my

The Kid in Purple Pants

Structured Approaches to Educating Underprivileged Students

friends about what he did. He said he had even sold houses to some of the parents of kids in my class. He wrote on the chalkboard and showed us that we needed to learn math in order to determine how much a new homeowner would have to pay for a new house. I was very proud that he was a "smart" dad who was not nervous and talked to us with sincere eyes and made us laugh at some of his jokes.

Some might argue that there is nothing that could top your dad coming to school for a treasured memory. Well, they would be wrong. The one thing better than having my Dad come to school with me was getting to wear those glorious, old, worn-out, probably stained, and useless soccer uniforms. My friends and I were privileged to wear Mrs. Kravenak's sons' soccer jerseys when we played soccer at recess. She and her husband were soccer fanatics and had coached their own boys' teams for years. She was kind enough to bring in the uniforms and allow us to wear them during our many versions of the World Cup. We felt like professionals and even had a special jersey for the goalie to wear.

By now, you might be wondering what all of this has to do with being a poor kid, and further, how it relates to educating poor children. Well, everything. My experiences in school, to this point, had been perfect. I had been taught to be intrinsically motivated. My teachers were happy and loved teaching. I had never been made to feel inferior to anyone, and I was taught that if I worked hard I could be whatever I wanted to be when I grew up. And, maybe most important, my two older brothers were the toughest kids in both St. Bernard's and Lewis and Clark Elementary. I had no fear. My brothers had my back and no one ever messed with me. My learning environment was exactly what every child needs— love, kindness, laughter, and security. If there is any other person in the world who can say the first five years of his/her

The Kid in Purple Pants

Structured Approaches to Educating Underprivileged Students

formal education were *more* enlightening, secure, thought-provoking, and happy as mine, he/she is one very lucky person.

Then, Not So Perfect Anymore

My happy existence at St. Bernard's started to change during fifth grade. I guess I had never had a bad teacher until then. In fact, I had loved all my teachers until about two weeks into my new school year. I had cherished how each of my previous teachers had cared about me and would laugh at the silly things I would say. They would retell the stories to other teachers in the hallway and would laugh and give me a smiling glance.

But things changed in fifth grade. My teacher no longer was the person I most wanted to please and make proud. She was no longer the individual I wanted to make laugh and show I was an original. She would degrade me and other students in my class. For the first time in my life, I thought that maybe I wasn't as smart as I had previously believed. I had always felt smart and was told I was so by all my teachers. I thought that trying your hardest and doing the best you could was what school was all about. That's what all my other teachers had thought too. Well, I guess we were wrong. My fifth-grade teacher got frustrated with us very easily, degraded us, and had teacher's pets. She made everything a competition, and would insult us. This humiliating talk cut deep, and I remember that I wasn't the only one who didn't like it. For the first time in our lives, my classmates and I wanted to be mean to our teacher.

I still remember Vince (the same Vince from kindergarten) telling me that if he heard how the teacher's kids were smarter than us just one more time he was going to steal all of

The Kid in Purple Pants

Structured Approaches to Educating Underprivileged Students

her markers. Before the end of that week, all her markers were gone. I loved and admired Vince for having the guts to teach her what we thought was a well-deserved lesson.

Fifth grade was also when I found out I was poor. I knew there was no Santa Claus and that my parents bought our Christmas presents. I recognized that other kids in my class received more toys than I did for Christmas and that was because their parents had more money. I understood that my family was large and my Mom didn't work because my younger siblings were not yet in school (she did eventually work the midnight shift as a waitress at IHOP during the late 1970s). So, we didn't have a ton of money. No big deal. I was well-adjusted and even understood that I was probably lucky to have so many siblings, because some of my friends didn't and wished they did.

Jason was a good friend who was an only child. He practically lived at my house. He would ride his bike over, and even if I weren't home he would spend the day playing with my little brother and sister. He didn't care; it was being part of a family that he enjoyed. He loved having someone to wrestle with, play tag with, and eat with, and someone he could teach how to ride a bike. (Jason still brags that one of his greatest accomplishments in life was teaching my little brother how to ride a two-wheeler.)

And then there was the Lavite family, which included my friends Misty and Vince. Being part of a large family, the kids got about the same as we did for Christmas. They played tag, dodgeball, and hide-and-seek. They didn't go to the movies or roller-skating, just like us. So, not having money? No big deal!

But finding out that friends in my class had noticed that I wore the same shirt and the same purple pants every day was something I will never forget.

The Kid in Purple Pants

Structured Approaches to Educating Underprivileged Students

We played soccer almost every day. And it wasn't that we had a bad physical education teacher. On the contrary, the P.E. teacher played with us, was young, was up for anything, and actually made us a competitive little group of kids. Although we would plead with her each and every day to play soccer, she would force us to play other sports such as volleyball and softball from time to time. But we would beg her to let us play soccer. Why did we want to play soccer every day? We had the "cage," an old 15-foot-high fenced-in tennis court that had the net and poles taken down. It made the perfect "outside indoor soccer field." That cage, unfortunately, is also where my enlightenment occurred, after a soccer game that, I guess now as I look back, my team must have won.

Billy was a very wealthy kid in our class whose dad owned a large company in town. His dad's company had a fleet of nice, new pick-up trucks with his surname spelled out in fancy cursive lettering on the side, and gigantic work trailers with the same elaborate lettering parked around town on job sites of the biggest construction projects in the county.

Billy must have been mad about the loss in that day's soccer game. As we were putting away our coats he looked over at me and said, "At least I don't wear the same shirt to school every day." I was stunned. I did wear the same shirt to school almost every day. It was the shirt I liked better of the two I owned. I was not the smallest fifth-grader (I had put on a few pounds since being the nimble kid in third grade), so my other shirt was always popping a button off at the belly, which is why I didn't wear it much. The shirt that I mostly wore was a little different, too. It was a shirt given to my Mom by my uncle, Allen. It was light blue and had a white collar. The school uniform called for a light blue or white shirt and dark blue dress pants. Well, I guess no one ever really cared that "technically" I was out of uniform with my white-collared light

The Kid in Purple Pants

Structured Approaches to Educating Underprivileged Students

blue shirt. At least I thought no one cared until Billy spoke up that day. I barked for him to shut up and said that I didn't wear the same shirt every day. He knew he had me. "Yes it is," he pressed, "it's got a white collar and you wear it every freaking day, Pat, we all know it." We all know it? Is that what he said? Everyone knew I wore the same shirt every day? I knew that wearing the same shirt every day was nothing to be proud of, but I hadn't realized it was something that everyone "knew." Why would they "know"? What did that mean? Did it mean I was different? Was that a bad thing? The other shirt was always missing a button; if someone would have asked, I would have explained that to them. Even the girls "knew"?

I wanted revenge and started making fun of his short stature and the fact that he couldn't drop kick a soccer ball to save his life. I was mad, embarrassed, and hurt as I tried to save face in front of my other friends, who were trying hard to divert their eyes from my frantic attempts to make eye contact with someone who would say Billy was wrong. He was mad about losing a soccer game and was trying to figure out a way to hurt me. It was a tactic a fifth-grader would use; he meant nothing by it. He was my friend. But a kid doesn't understand that when he is 10 years old.

It wasn't until I became an adult that I realized how monumental that day was in my life. I look back on that day and see that many of the insecurities I have had (and probably still have) were a direct reflection of that day. I never knew that anyone would care that I wore the same shirt to school each day or that it would ever be the topic of someone's discussion.

From that day forward, I despised having to wear the same clothes and did everything in my power never to wear the same shirt or pants two days in a row. This was compli-

The Kid in Purple Pants

Structured Approaches to Educating Underprivileged Students

cated by the fact that my school uniform pants were purple. The uniform called for dark blue pants, but for some reason my "new" school pants, which happened to also be my everything pants, had been bleached and were now more purple than blue. I have no idea how they could have gotten bleached, but they did. They were the only pair of pants I had. My mother was heartbroken that they had been ruined but she was powerless to do anything about it. It wasn't like they had a big hole in them and couldn't be worn. They were just purple.

I hated wearing those pants because I knew I had to wear them EVERY day and everyone could tell the pants were just like the shirt, my EVERYDAY pants. No one ever said anything about those purple pants, and I think I know why. I was also one of the tougher boys in my class and I know they understood I had a chip on my shoulder about being chubby and poor. Not that any of them, other than Vince, understood what it was like to be poor, but they did comprehend how a kid could react to situations in which money was an issue.

Finding out that I was poor and could possibly be someone's object of ridicule was difficult and caused me to sometimes want to skip school when I knew that wearing the same clothes two days in a row was inevitable.

To complicate matters, I really dreaded "blue jeans" day, those special occasions when we were allowed to wear jeans to school. Not having to wear our uniform was cause for celebration and was the talk of the school the entire week before our day of reprieve. The only problem was that I didn't own any blue jeans. I would be forced to wear my purple pants and pretend that I "forgot" that we could wear blue jeans. How in the world does a kid forget to wear blue jeans on those rare and precious few opportunities when he was allowed to wear them? It was unfathomable, and certainly unbelievable. It

The Kid in Purple Pants

Structured Approaches to Educating Underprivileged Students

bothered me so much that I resorted to pretending I was sick with a stomachache on St. Patrick's Day. No one, and I mean no one, ever missed school on St. Patrick's Day. It was the greatest day of the year for St. Bernard's students. We played carnival games, ate pizza, drank soda, and had raffles and a cakewalk—complete and utter joy for a child. But, because jeans were the dress code on St. Patrick's Day, I didn't want to go to school in purple pants and feign forgetfulness again.

I know it may seem odd, having these issues at a private Catholic school where everyone supposedly wore the same clothes. Even under those circumstances, kids notice when you are different, and it ultimately influences your self-image and the way you perceive yourself and the rest of the world.

Did I only have one day in my life when I felt bad about my economic situation? Of course not. I kept growing. And as I did, the situations became more obvious to others and visible to me. I wore Kmart-brand tennis shoes, which I accidentally tore up while trying to make them look like a pair of Adidas. I bought all my clothes at Dollar General, played sports when I could afford the required apparel, and so on. I could write an entire book about the different, awkward situations my siblings and I dealt with because of our unique situation.

One of my favorite memories of childhood is when my big brother got a new pair of shoes. It was the summer of my sixth-grade year and my oldest brother Harry was roofing for my Dad's company. It was a Friday, and Harry must have been paid for his week's work (something that was not always guaranteed). Harry came home from the mall with a brand new pair of leather Nikes. They were perfect. They didn't just "look" like a pair of Nikes either; they *were* Nikes. I was so proud of those shoes. They were exactly like the neighbor's, who had never worked one day in his entire life but got everything he wanted.

The Kid in Purple Pants

Structured Approaches to Educating Underprivileged Students

We went to school with kids who were very much middle- and upper middle-class boys and girls. Our friends' and classmates' parents worked at McDonnell Douglas (now known as Boeing), owned big construction companies, or were barge ship captains. I wouldn't change a thing about my childhood, but along with my Mom's need to see us happy, our unique situation fostered in my siblings and me a longing to be successful.

Poor Kids Need Help

So, why write a book about childhood stuff that that only a therapist should hear? Because we had something else going for us: Not all poor kids are as lucky as the Anderson clan. All poor kids have similar experiences. But not all had a mom and a dad like my siblings and I did. We were some of the luckiest kids in the world. We had parents who believed in us and made us feel that no matter what happened to us, we were never to let someone make us feel inferior. Our parents were smart enough to know that each of their children was fighting his or her own battles in some way, and understood their job was to foster in us a will to achieve, no matter what precon- ceived notions existed about us. No crazy nun or pompous high school counselor was allowed to make us feel as though we were second-class citizens.

Still, we fought lots of physical and mental battles. My oldest brother, probably one of the skinniest kids in all Wood River during the late 1970s, was also the toughest kid in both the public school and St. Bernard's. Why? He wouldn't allow anyone to degrade him. He took every opportunity to kick the holy hell out of whoever tried to make him, or any of his little brothers or sister, feel they were not just as smart or capable as anyone else.

The Kid in Purple Pants

Structured Approaches to Educating Underprivileged Students

I was lucky. I had a drive and a commitment to family instilled in me that not many poor students get. There was no hiding the fact that the Anderson brood stuck together. I guess you could also say that everything I needed to know I learned from being told repeatedly, "You don't fight with your brothers and sister. When you grow up, they will be your best friends," and, "I don't care what your brother does, you never ever take someone else's side in a fight or an argument." My Mom's words ring in my ears to this day and if I ever have to hide a body, my youngest brother will be the first person I call. The only question he will ask is whether he needs to bring a shovel. My parents taught us that if we share, it would ultimately make us all better and stronger. And this is why I know I have been able to battle through the difficulties I was dealt as a youngster, to flourish as an adult.

I had a family that loved me and cared for me and didn't allow outside influences and psychological scars to manipulate how I ultimately saw myself. But my situation is the exception, not the rule. A life of self-pity and anger would seem a more reasonable end to my childhood. My parents could have easily given up and taught us the survival skills that many poor children learn from their parents. Some learn a sense of entitlement and how to look to others to solve their problems. Many learn that giving up is easier and that, ultimately, you will survive. This is the road map to adulthood that many underprivileged students follow every day in schools across America.

It is imperative that we take note of the distinctive circumstances that so many students face and find a method for providing an education that permits students to be whatever they choose to be, not what they feel they should be based on where they come from and what they have experienced. We must create an approach to educating all our students that

The Kid in Purple Pants

Structured Approaches to Educating Underprivileged Students

guarantees those who don't have tough older brothers, a mother with a vision, and a father with conviction can also make their way through our public education system with a yearning to achieve and be whatever it is they choose to become.

Writing about the joys of kindergarten, a pretty teacher, a father's visit to a son's class, and a chubby fifth-grader wearing purple pants will not help bring about logical changes in the way we meet the needs of our dispossessed students.

Let's change focus in this book. Let's see new ways that schools can address the requirements of their poorest students. Let's discuss the philosophical approaches, initiatives, programs, best practices, and professional development used to impart the best schooling to our students. Knowing an approach that has seen positive outcomes may help to give surety that other students will have a fighting chance at getting to do what they want in life. And what is that? Being happy. The type of happiness that is only afforded to those who are enjoying every day of their lives by doing what they love.

Who knows, maybe some truly happy kid will wear the brightest purple pants in the world.

The Kid in Purple Pants

Structured Approaches to Educating Underprivileged Students

Those born into poverty or on the margins of society require our extra support to realize their dreams.

Novak Djokovic

Chapter 2

How Do You Forget You're Poor?

"Being poor is having to live with choices you didn't know
you made when you were 14 years old."

—John Scalzi

I am fortunate that I already knew what I wanted to do with my life by the time I was a sophomore in high school. I read the poem "Thanatopsis" by William Cullen Bryant and from that day on I knew I wanted to teach and share with others my love of literature, poetry, and the English language. Nothing excited me more than expressing to young people what novels and poems could do for the soul. So I went to college, got my degree, landed my first job, and forgot that I had been a poor kid.

My first job was in the small farm town of Oakland, Illinois. The students were well-behaved, polite, and loved sports. Many were the children of the working poor.

I thought I was the greatest teacher in the world. I really did. I had no idea just how bad I was at teaching. Yet I loved my job. I had a couple of junior high classes and the rest were high school English and literature courses.

I was getting paid to teach. I really didn't know many people, other than my two older brothers, who had a job where you didn't have to sweat to make money. I had been a roofer all my life, and when you roof for a living, everything after that is cake. By the time I began high school, my father

The Kid in Purple Pants

Structured Approaches to Educating Underprivileged Students

had stopped selling real estate and our family roofing company was the way we made a living. We worked hard. I want to write another book one day titled *Whatever I Didn't Learn in Kindergarten Was Figured Out on a Roof.* Although the work was exhausting and dirty and the heat was overwhelming, the pride of completing a hard day's work can't be topped.

But now teaching was providing a paycheck (granted, I took home $1,100 a month in 1993). There was nothing in the world I would have rather been doing. I was also head golf coach. I had lied during the interview and told the high school principal that I was a scratch golfer with experience giving lessons and helping out at the local public course. The head golf coach position paid an extra $700 a year and there was no way I was going to pass up the opportunity to make a little extra money by simply playing golf with a bunch of high school boys. No school officials ever found out that I had lied. Actually, the only people who ever knew were the male colleagues I golfed with and the guys who worked at the course. We were a young faculty going out together, drinking, and having a good time.

When I say that I was a bad teacher, it is meant in the context that I wasn't a good teacher for those poor students who needed me most. Actually, I was good at teaching figurative language, direct objects, split infinitives, and preparing students for state tests. But I was clueless as to what it took to reach those students who were struggling the most. I was a typical high school/junior high teacher.

"You need to come prepared."

"Forget something and it's a zero."

"Don't ever give me some lame excuse. I don't want to hear it."

The Kid in Purple Pants

Structured Approaches to Educating Underprivileged Students

Those lines were part of my repertoire. I'm not proud of what I was, but I must admit that was how I ran my classroom. For those students who were responsible, had structure in their lives, and came to school prepared to learn, I was great. For everyone else, which happened to be a large percentage of my students, I was not the teacher I thought I was. I thought that because many of my students who did my homework and performed well on my tests were "getting" what I was teaching, I was a high-quality teacher. I never once sat back and thought that maybe I would *really* be a first-rate teacher if I could find a way to reach the students who didn't do homework or perform well on tests. How could have I forgotten what it was like for them? I had even given rides home to some of my students and saw the condition of the houses in which they were living. How was I unable to perceive that in all the same ways, these students were wearing purple pants and despising going to school? I was doing what every new teacher does when given his or her first job. I was surviving.

Paul was one of the most challenging students I ever had. He was a class clown and would ask the dumbest questions, never pay attention, and was constantly trying to find a way to be the center of attention. He drove me absolutely batty. He could throw the entire class off track, and because I didn't have the skills to stop him, I would yell and intimidate him. I know now that what Paul was really doing was trying to figure out a way to keep everyone from noticing that his clothes were filthy dirty, he received free lunch, and that he never had his homework finished even though he was a smart kid.

One day I was forced to give Paul a ride home after he served a detention. No one could come pick him up, the bus routes had all been run, and he lived about three miles outside of town. I recall that the ride home with Paul was not that bad. He actually talked like a normal human being, listened when I

The Kid in Purple Pants

Structured Approaches to Educating Underprivileged Students

talked, and was polite. The kid starving for attention and needing to make sure no one knew he was poor didn't have an audience of peers to impress. I can still see his house as clearly as I did almost 20 years ago.

It was more of a shack than a home. The porch had a five-gallon bucket standing in for the steps. A huge blue tarp covered half the roof, and the rest must have still been leaking. Two cars with flat tires and obviously not in working condition were parked in the front yard. An old crash-up derby car with the numbers "00" spray-painted on the side was parked in the backyard. It hurt me to see where Paul lived and I am sure he was embarrassed for me to see it. But did it change the way I saw Paul? Did it make me stop and wonder whether Paul saw any use in going to school and doing his best? Did it make me question whether this skinny kid was getting enough to eat? No. The next day Paul was back to his old ways. I was frustrated and remember thinking that he was just "poor white trash" and couldn't be saved. Why couldn't I connect with my struggling students? Hadn't I been embarrassed by the shabby furniture in my home? Hadn't I roofed with some of the poorest and most hopeless and disenfranchised young men as an adolescent? Yes, I had. But because I thought what I was doing was the single most important thing in the world, I lost sight of the fact that what I was doing wasn't really all that important at all.

Also, I had enough money to pay for a flat tire if I got one, take my wife out to eat, and cover my mortgage. I had started a family and my new daughter was the center of my universe. My basic needs were being met, so nothing was more important to me than making certain I was giving my all to producing the best English-speaking students in the world. Having everyone turn in their essays on *Huckleberry Finn* was my top priority, but it certainly wasn't a top priority for

The Kid in Purple Pants

Structured Approaches to Educating Underprivileged Students

my student whose father was in jail and whose mom was never home to help her feed and take care of her little brother.

As I look back at those days with the wisdom I have been able to acquire as a veteran teacher and administrator, I have many regrets. The slightest bit of professional development during my early teaching career, an initiative that focused on meeting the needs of the poor, or a workshop on how to teach struggling students might have helped. I now realize that I wasn't as bright as I thought I was at age 24.

My wife and I moved back to Wood River after I spent four years teaching in central Illinois. I landed a job in O'Fallon, Illinois. A total of 63% of my students were in economic hardship and almost 15% of them were considered homeless, yet I could think of nothing other than that I had given up my tenure in Oakland and I was scared to death of losing my new job. Testing, as I remember it, was a top priority. A teacher's ability to keep his or her job was based on test scores. My wife and I wanted to have a second child and money had become a very important commodity. I was even stricter with my students and made certain that not a one of them stepped out of line or gave cause to pay attention to my teaching skills. I took pride in having the best-behaved classes. When I had a substitute, I could scare my students into behaving just as well as they would for me.

Was I all bad? I don't believe so. Like I said before, when it comes to preparing students for high-stakes, mandated state tests, I am the man. I can take a curriculum and teach it from the inside out. I could have every student understand all the literary devices, read for a main idea, and distinguish between irony and just bad luck, which is no easy task. But, was I doing anything to help the kids who were not turning in homework, not studying for tests, or not participating in class?

The Kid in Purple Pants

Structured Approaches to Educating Underprivileged Students

27

It wasn't until I became a principal, after almost 15 years as a classroom teacher, that I realized my teaching skills were deficient. It took looking in from the outside and discovering I was a narcissist so full of myself that I had totally forgotten why, as a child, sometimes I hadn't wanted to go to school and why sometimes I got behind in my schoolwork. As a teacher I only cared about what my ISAT (Illinois Standards Achievement Test) scores were going to be and whether I was going to get an "attaboy" from my principal for raising scores and doing better than our neighboring district with all the "rich kids." Because I was concerned for my own well-being, I had put myself into survival mode:

1. Make sure you don't do anything that could jeopardize your job;

2. Don't send any kids to the office; principals hate that!, and

3. Don't end up broke!

This is all I kept hearing in my head as I maintained order and stuck to the script. Does it sound like a poor kid turned adult and a father wanting to protect himself from his past? You bet.

I should defend myself a little. I wasn't as cold-hearted and cruel as that sounds. When students' needs were *very* obvious, I was the first to give them what they needed. A kid with no lunch money—no problem. A kid without a coat—I would find a coat. Those things were easy fixes that I could remedy with a few dollars or by looking through the back of my closet. I was starting to change and had no idea. The exposure to character education and the positive effects that it has on children and learning was starting to rub off.

The Kid in Purple Pants

Structured Approaches to Educating Underprivileged Students

I was also smart and lucky enough to finally get a little professional development about the differences between rich kids and poor kids.

Oh, What a Little Training Can Do

When I first met the principal, I thought he was a lunatic who only cared about test scores. But he turned out to be different than what I thought. Steve Amizich did care about test scores and about beating the "rich kids" in District 90, but he ultimately cared most about helping kids who did not have the skills needed to be successful in school.

Steve had introduced character education to Central School District #104. And boy, did it need it. "There were some tough, tough kids in this school who only knew how to have a knock-down, drag-out fight to solve a problem," Steve says now, with a grin and a firm shaking of his head. "If I wasn't in the lunch room right when that bell rang, there was, sure as hell, going to be a fight."

My last two years of being a classroom teacher was when I first learned about Ruby Payne and her research on poverty. I was dreading going to another useless in-service where I would have to listen to someone preach about how to be a better teacher, and who would try to make us laugh at some lame jokes, and then have to eat some hideous school food service lunch because the administrators were afraid if we were allowed to get lunch on our own we would never come back. This was my mindset as a large African-American woman named Dr. Rita Pierson came onto the stage and started to speak.

I was mesmerized. Holy crap, I thought, this woman was talking about me! She discussed why poor kids fight. As a kid, I wanted to fight all the time when I got mad. My broth-

.

The Kid in Purple Pants

Structured Approaches to Educating Underprivileged Students

29

ers *did* fight when they were mad. She talked about why people in poverty sometimes buy things that are too expensive and that they cannot afford. I liked expensive clothes that I could not afford. Now that I had a real job, I loved Ralph Lauren and would not buy anything name-brand if it did not have the name or symbol on the outside of it so that everyone could admire it. This woman talked about how middle class people were different than poor people. Holy crap, again! That was my wife. She had grown up middle class. She wanted to save money, use coupons, and cook at home instead of going out to eat. She loved bargains and would shop for two days to save a nickel on a gallon of milk. She didn't care about brand names as an adult and was already thinking about our daughter's college fund! Our daughter was only a baby, for Pete's sake! The speaker even talked about how being an entertainer was of value in a home of poverty. I thought of my former student, Paul. He was pretty funny now that I thought about it. I reflected back to my own family sitting in our home and each of us trying to be the funniest person in the room on hot summer nights when we had no air conditioning and were simply trying not to think about the oppressive heat.

As Dr. Pierson went on, I laughed until my sides ached. She was hilarious and her stories were dead-on for me. I recall my face hurting from smiling so much and thinking back to everything I had ever experienced. I nodded my head and for the first time in my life wanted to scream out, "Amen, sister!" I had learned a great deal about myself and was actually going to use something I had learned in an in-service. I realized that I needed to change how I was going forward.

Two years later, I became a principal. With my new position and the training I had received, reality started to sink in. I saw several reasons why students weren't engrossed in school. I understood the rationale for why homework wasn't

The Kid in Purple Pants

Structured Approaches to Educating Underprivileged Students

finished after my first parent conference in which the mother was strung out on methamphetamines. I quickly comprehended the benefits of not allowing a 13-year-old child the liberty of failing. Quickly I understood—with the help of a dear friend and extraordinary special education coordinator—that just because a kid is poor, depressed, and unmotivated doesn't mean he or she should be in special education. I learned what it was like to have a 14-year-old girl cry in my office because all she ever wanted was a little attention from anyone and she was now pregnant, scared, and had no one to turn to but me. It doesn't take long for a person to see situations for what they really are once that person gets his or her eyes opened. I can't say I noticed these things alone. What good fortune I have had throughout my career. Great colleagues and fellow leaders have always surrounded me. With the help of the school board, superintendent, counselor, and caring teachers, we raised the bar.

So, now that I had realized that my two Emerson Electric Excellence in Teaching Awards may have been warranted for my teaching ability, and not my ability to reach *all* children, I wanted to make certain I made no more mistakes when it came to helping those students who had the most need. I had experienced too much myself and realized that the kids who needed me the most were those that either hid in the back of class, said nothing, and were allowed to fall through the cracks, or were those students who used every outlandish coping skill they had to make sure that no one knew how they really felt and how they were truly struggling inside. I began to slowly realize what was needed. Caring and loving disadvantaged kids was simply not going to be enough. It was going to take a structured approach that utilized a philosophy where all students can be successful.

The Kid in Purple Pants

Structured Approaches to Educating Underprivileged Students

31

At Central School District #104, we were the trendsetters. There was no initiative we wouldn't try, no program we wouldn't implement. We had so much professional development and training that after only one year of being a principal, I was offered a position as an assistant superintendent in a neighboring district because I knew everything there was to know about curriculum mapping, scope and sequence, and Response to Intervention (RtI; techniques used in closing the achievement gap). What we were doing in education was working, for the most part, but there was no system or reason for when we did something or how we tried to steward these programs. We had too many irons in the fire to ever be great at one thing. Still, over the years we have focused our attention toward creating an approach that helps the neediest students. Has it been controversial? Sometimes. Has it been easy? Never. But it has made a world of difference in the lives of many of our students. Because we have become data driven and approach helping our students as a process, we have seen significant growth in those students. None of this, however, would have ever been possible if we had not decided we must have a true, systematic approach to teaching.

We Have Identified the Problem, So What Next?

Who should we blame for our current school system, which enables and seemingly encourages poor students to not be successful? There isn't one person or one group. But I'm sure that educators could easily find something or someone to point a finger at for the failures of our educational system. I know I have personally pointed the finger at the president, senators, governor, parents, politicians, superintendents, principals, fellow teachers, and even students. Is it helpful to do that? Not at all. So why waste our time reading about who

The Kid in Purple Pants

Structured Approaches to Educating Underprivileged Students

messed things up and how they were irresponsible and child-ish? Why listen to politicians blame one another for why our system is failing a large population of our society while at the same time telling us why they should be re-elected? It doesn't make sense and it doesn't change the fact that if poor kids are still being left behind it is because we do not take the neces-sary precautions to ensure that they do not fail.

Do I blame the parents of these children for not being like my parents? No. My parents could very well have been those exact people. Why were they different? I don't know. Maybe because they were two poor kids who were forced to be less than what they knew they could be. My Mom was encouraged to drop out of high school at age 16, but she was smart enough to get my Dad through his senior year and see him graduate high school. Maybe they just understood what they might have needed from their parents in order to do what they wanted. Ultimately, I think it was something that my Mom believed that may be the crucial reason that her five poor kids became happy adults. She would say, "All I care about is if you are happy. And to be happy, you need to pick what you do. If digging ditches will make you happy, then be the best ditch-digger in the world. But, if you want something else, then make sure you give yourself the opportunity to do it." She understood that if her children did what made them happy, they would be successful. How many people do you know who are at the top of their fields and yet are miserable in their jobs? How many of them are going above and beyond within their professions and doing new and ingenious things?

All parents want their children to be happy and success-ful. Do they all have the aptitude to teach their children the necessary skills for making happiness a reality? Not always. When parents have to put so much focus into just maintaining the rent and keeping food on the table, frustration, anger, and

The Kid in Purple Pants

Structured Approaches to Educating Underprivileged Students

resentment sometimes keep them from realizing what students need: encouragement, support, and love.

Do I blame the children? After all, shouldn't they see the benefits of an education? Shouldn't these students be smart enough to see that many of their families embody the stereotypical circle of poverty that plagues many societies? No, they don't. They are children. Children are innately a mess. That's not an insult. My son is a complete mess. He's 11 years old and is one of the funniest people I have ever met. But when he tells a story, it ultimately turns into an episode of *Tom and Jerry*. His mind goes a mile a minute and he jumps from thought to thought without missing a single beat. He knows exactly what he is trying to convey, but the rest of the world doesn't consist entirely of fifth-graders. (Incidentally, his friends have no problem understanding him.)

I speak often at school engagements, and one of my favorite requests is when I am asked to speak to "soon-to-be" middle school educators. These are the people, like me, who are just nuts enough to want to teach middle school students. They are the cream of the crop of teachers because they know what they are getting themselves into and still want to do it! I ask these soon-to-be teachers to describe a middle school student. It doesn't take long before adjectives start to fly from the mouths of these young educators. Scared, confused, self-conscious, nervous, easily embarrassed, angry, melancholy, fidgety, easily influenced, and hormonal are only the start of the list. After we finish the inventory, I again ask them whether they actually want to teach a group of people who are described this way. We all have a good laugh and realize that we must be very aware of our audience if we are to be successful educators. It is something that even the best teachers in the world sometimes forget.

The Kid in Purple Pants

Structured Approaches to Educating Underprivileged Students

Thus, why do we expect students who come from poor and impoverished homes to be as successful as those students who come from homes where their basic needs are met, their social and emotional needs are secure, and they have experienced the benefits of hard work and determination? It's because we live in a society where we are all expected to pull ourselves up by our bootstraps and be just as successful as the next guy no matter what influences or disadvantages might be holding us back. It's the American way. We admire and make heroes out of those who overcome adversity and beat the odds. There is no greater story than that of rags to riches.

Let me digress for a moment. I am no better than anyone else. I take every opportunity I get to brag about my siblings. They are the rags to riches (maybe not riches, but at least upper middle class, which is rich for a poor kid) story that everyone wants to hear about. The skinny older brother (Harry) who fought everyone who ever thought of ridiculing him is now a lawyer who spends most of his time in Mexico scuba diving and doing what my Mom told him to be (i.e., happy). Michael is a geologist and, although we cherish making fun of him for getting excited over limestone and slate, he loves his work. My lone sister is a self-described computer nerd who often works from home and enjoys every second of her life with her children, nieces, and nephews. She listened to mom, too. And my brother Kyle will always be the "baby." He is the youngest-ever elected city councilman in Wood River. Who would have thought that the top vote-getter in the last council election would have been one of the Anderson kids? He is the pride of the Democratic Party in Madison County, Illinois. Every laborer, electrician, county official, state representative, and civic leader in three counties adores Kyle. Nothing brings him more joy than knowing that his work has kept someone's electricity turned on, or that his efforts have enabled a

The Kid in Purple Pants

Structured Approaches to Educating Underprivileged Students

neighborhood to no longer suffer from dilapidated storm drains that cause their basements to flood. All in all, I'd say it's a pretty good return on my parents' investment.

Is this digression part of the problem? We become fascinated by the idea of overcoming hardship and lose sight of a means of alleviating those hardships so that all can succeed. Why not create an approach to educating disadvantaged students that focuses on creating success, self-pride, determination, and responsibility while at the same time meeting the academic needs that all people need to do great things? Isn't that all any human being needs to accomplish personal goals and live a happy life? It is not a difficult concept.

Fifty years ago the idea of instructing students with special needs in differentiated methods, unique environments, distinctive curriculums, and altered time frames was unimaginable. I remember more than once my own father stating that in the 1950s, it was believed that kids weren't "special," they were just "stupid." A kid who struggled was just not trying hard enough rather than requiring extra instruction. My father is no special education guru, but even he could see as a 1950s adolescent that the problems facing the most in-need students were not being met.

However, something amazing happened for our students with special needs. The advocates for these children persisted and their learning environment is being altered and made better every day. Books, seminars, conventions, budgets, and even entire legislative sessions (state and federal) have been devoted to improving the needs of students who have cognitive, psychological, mental, and emotional needs. Is it because the needs of these children are more visible and easily seen by the public eye? Perhaps. The issues of our students with special needs are more obvious than those of the ones who try to hide their shame about needing extra help. It took a genuine

The Kid in Purple Pants

Structured Approaches to Educating Underprivileged Students

effort by a concerned group of individuals, parents, and activists to bring about change that all people now know, understand, and accept as truth. The needs of special education students cannot be addressed in the conventional school setting that existed in public schools. Nevertheless, this same mantra has not been accepted for meeting the needs of the poor.

Would we ever allow for school buildings to be designed and erected without the proper accessibility for those with disabilities? Can you imagine a school bathroom without stalls for wheelchair access or an auditorium built without ramps? It would be a travesty and cause for public outrage and anger. An administrator or architect who overlooked such a huge aspect of a building project would be immediately fired and humiliated for his or her inability to distinguish something that is so obviously needed. And for too long the needs of poor students have been subject to the benevolence of attentive teachers and administrators. It's not enough. Educators must be the advocates for the poor. We see firsthand the effects of poverty on learning and still have not been successful in helping bring about real change. Helping poor students only when it's obvious is not going to bring about the changes we need or do anything to close the achievement gaps that grow as the number of poor people increases.

The Kid in Purple Pants

Structured Approaches to Educating Underprivileged Students

37

No man can tell whether he is rich or poor by turning to his ledger. It is the heart that makes a man rich. He is rich or poor according to what he is, not according to what he has.

Henry Ward Beecher

The Kid in Purple Pants

Structured Approaches to Educating Underprivileged Students

Chapter 3

Are Poor Kids Different?

"The secret of education lies in respecting the pupil."

—Ralph Waldo Emerson

Are poor kids different? From whom? From the average, middle-class student who attends public school. "Different" may not be the exact word, but to me it seems the most appropriate word to convey that poor students come to school with distinctive expectations, uncertainties, and preconceived notions about learning, and they are vastly different from those of other students.

Good teachers across the world adhere to the notion that all children are capable of learning and succeeding no matter what the challenges might be. That notion is the sign of a good teacher. We all want to believe we can fix every child who walks through our classroom door. We all know that if we can just show them the importance of what we are trying to teach them, they will have no choice but to become completely enamored by our methods and us and what we say will trump their preconceived notions about school.

Unfortunately, this is not usually the case, nor do we have a magic wand that allows us to rid many of our poor children from believing that living in poverty is the only existence they will ever know. That mindset is hard to change for poor children. Still, if we as educators continue to feel that, by giving out enough zeroes and the right number of detentions, things

The Kid in Purple Pants

Structured Approaches to Educating Underprivileged Students

39

will ultimately change and all the children will become perfect students. If that were only so! Our present approach to education simply doesn't work for "different" kids. But these approaches work for those for whom they were developed: students who are motivated, challenged, and have guidance and a goal in mind. The education system works for those who see education as a thing of value. This is not to imply that value in education cannot be taught and learned, but in our present system, it doesn't work for all.

Why doesn't the system work for "different" kids? Because America's educational structure was flawed at its inception. During the 19th and 20th centuries our industrial model for education was designed to prepare the majority of young people for factory work. It allowed and even encouraged students to drop out of school and get a job. But today's educators should, rather, be focused on giving all students a chance at success at learning. If the student gets an even chance (with support, encouragement, and guidance), should that person then leave to work, that's fine.

There is also no scripted answer to teaching, and anyone who tries to convince you otherwise is completely clueless. Teaching is an art. And much like the skills of a carpenter, the art is honed and the crafts are mastered and refined throughout a teacher's career. Taking away a teacher's ability to learn these skills stifles creativity and minimizes the capacity to capitalize on experience and mentoring. Think how difficult it would be to identify a "teacher of the year" candidate if we all followed a scripted model for teaching. I can almost hear the announcer saying,

> *"This year's award goes to no one. None of us has tried anything outside the box in an attempt to differ-*

The Kid in Purple Pants

Structured Approaches to Educating Underprivileged Students

entiate instruction or meet the needs of a struggling student."

Can you imagine asking a physician or a lawyer to treat every patient or client exactly the same way and to not capitalize on his or her experience and knowledge?

Likewise, a script for helping poor kids change their mindset does not exist. The ability to help underprivileged children succeed is a case-by-case endeavor because each student brings to the table his or her own unique situation. Teachers can't afford to pretend that a student who might be hungry, stressed, humiliated, apathetic, or simply dirty will be able to concentrate, learn, and thrive in the same way as other students. We must not fool ourselves into thinking that everyone is equally capable of flourishing under the same circumstances.

Though I made some bad mistakes during my tenure as a teacher, I could still distinguish which teachers were completely out of touch and which teachers "had it together." I knew that all kids were different, unique, and trying to find their own niche or path. I also knew the first time I heard the words "kids these days" uttered from the mouth of angry, upset, or frustrated teachers, they were fooling themselves into thinking their lack of ability was somehow the students' fault. I acknowledged, even as a first-year teacher, that a kid is a kid and there was no difference between the students of the 1950s and those of the 1990s.

Don't get me wrong: I understood the difference in technology, social influences, and economic hardship and how those manipulate human development. But in the '50s we had students who were spoiled, angry, confused, and mischievous, which really is no different from students in the '90s. Students from both generations would sneak gum in class, act out when

The Kid in Purple Pants

Structured Approaches to Educating Underprivileged Students

they were bored, and were even, heaven forbid, sometimes disrespectful to teachers. It was a reality that I knew because I saw myself in many of the boys in my classes. I recognized that my seniors were just as enamored by girls as I was at 18 years old, and that the 14-year-olds were just as confused about everything that was happening to them as I had been. In reality, there is no hiding the fact that biological changes in adolescent boys have not changed in the last 40 years, and that teachers today are facing the same challenges of yesteryear.

Yet it seemed that not everyone understood these concepts, as I discovered one day during my third year of teaching. As I ate my lunch in the teachers' lounge, a fellow teacher, who was never happy and hated her position, started in on how bad all the eighth-graders were and that "kids these days" had no respect. I was tired of hearing these types of comments, so I said (in my best "I'm trying to make a point" voice), "One time in eighth grade, Brian Lavite [Vince's little brother] peed in the science lab drawer in our classroom." Everyone in the lounge froze. Some of my teacher friends whom I had confided in about how this woman just didn't "get it" started shaking their heads as if to tell me, "No, Pat, don't." I continued, "My Dad told me about how he and his brother threw cherry bombs down the hallway during summer school back in 1961." And I concluded with my favorite, "My grandpa told me about how he and his friends, in 1924, put a snake in the outhouse right before the teacher went in to use it."

Everyone else in the lounge sat wide-eyed and silent, waiting for Mrs. Neverhappy to respond. Having gotten my point, they were uneasy because my comments were so blatantly directed at her commentary that they thought there was

The Kid in Purple Pants

Structured Approaches to Educating Underprivileged Students

about to be a war of words, followed by an attack with rock-hard grilled cheese sandwiches and tomato soup.

But there was no war. She had no clue that I was making a point. She simply rolled her eyes and walked out of the lounge, still angry at some eighth-grader who had left his book bag in the hallway for the second day in a row. Imagine!

What that teacher and administrators sometimes forget is that all students are not made from the same mold, and we are the ones who have been charged with discovering their nuances and finding a way to capitalize on them for the betterment of their education. My colleague didn't consider that perhaps this student wasn't aware of a rule, was very hungry and wanted to be first in line for lunch, or maybe he was just one of those kids who just didn't care. She just assumed that he was disrespectful and was going out of his way to make his teachers—at least her—angry. I know thousands of eighth-graders and, trust me, they can think of many more things to make me angry than leaving a book bag in the hallway.

Poor children bring a plethora of social norms and stereotypical beliefs foreign to the average schoolteacher. Is it any wonder that many teachers find it hard to relate to their students and have difficulty understanding the barriers that some of them might be facing?

The Average Student Is Not the Average Teacher

A total of 75% of American teachers are white females who were raised in a middle-class environment. They are married with children and are able to save a small percentage of their income while at the same time paying into a pension system. Compare that with a child who has never known his father, has never been inside a bank, and doesn't know what a pension is. This divide makes it difficult for a teacher to realize

The Kid in Purple Pants

Structured Approaches to Educating Underprivileged Students

that a poor student would rather lie about why he doesn't have his homework finished than admit that the electricity was turned off and there was no light for him to be able to see to read or write. Teachers who were raised middle class find it hard, because of their own upbringing, not to mistake ignorance and disenfranchisement for laziness and apathy.

This story helps to illustrate my point. DeAudra was an extremely intelligent seventh-grader who happened to be a foster child. She had been taken away from her biological mother because, at the time, she had been living in a car. Since I knew this about her, I watched out for DeAudra. I wanted to make sure every one of her needs was being met at school. I made sure her lunch was free. I made certain her teachers knew to watch out for any signs of depression or anxiety. I even made sure the counselor had a weekly talk with her to see how she was progressing. But I didn't know one very important fact about African-American girls and their hair.

One day, DeAudra walked into the cafeteria for breakfast wearing a stocking cap. She didn't seem like her ordinary self that morning, but that didn't mean I was going to let her wear a hat in school. We have never allowed students to wear hats and it had never been a big issue. But DeAudra's reaction when I asked her to please take off her hat was much different than mild resistance or a rolling of her eyes. She immediately turned her back on me and ignored what I had said. I was a little surprised. DeAudra was a great kid. She must not have heard me. Again, I repeated the order to take off her hat. Nothing. This time she didn't even turn her back on me, she just stared at me like I was a complete and utter idiot. Please don't misunderstand me. I have been given that look many times, from my own children, teachers, principals, and people who know me fairly well. But this was different. DeAudra

The Kid in Purple Pants

Structured Approaches to Educating Underprivileged Students

was looking at me with eyes that shouted, "You are really doing this to me?"

By this time, my request for DeAudra to take off her hat and her refusal to do so were getting the attention of half the kids in the cafeteria. I started to panic. This hadn't happened to me since my second or third year of teaching. A kid not listening to Mr. Anderson? It just didn't happen. I was the *principal*. What was she thinking? To save face, I walked straight over to DeAudra and raised my voice.

"DeAudra, make me tell you one more time to take off that hat and we are going to the office!" I said, hoping it was my best *God, I hope she hadn't heard me the other times, but I have to sound tough* voice.

DeAudra didn't flinch. She turned around, crossed her arms with conviction, and yelled back, "NO!" What could I do? Without missing a beat, I screamed, "Get to the office, NOW!"

DeAudra stomped off to the office and, as I followed her, stomping just as hard, I noticed that she had started to cry. She needs to be crying, I tried to tell myself. She hadn't listened to me. For god's sake, I had asked her three times. If I didn't get tough with her, every kid in the school would be wearing a stocking cap tomorrow morning. As I continued to stomp behind her, I was trying to convince myself I hadn't just made a big mistake.

DeAudra slammed open my office door and slung herself into a chair. I stormed in right behind and screeched, "What in the world is wrong with you?" Nothing again, just looking straight down at the floor with tears flowing from her eyes. "DeAudra, look at me," I said, this time with concern in my voice. Detecting my tone, she looked me in the eye and waited for me to continue. "What's the deal? It's a hat, DeAudra. I didn't ask you to chop your arm off."

The Kid in Purple Pants

Structured Approaches to Educating Underprivileged Students

No explanation came forth. This was going to be a lot harder than I thought. I walked out of the office and went to retrieve my coffee cup. I knew we both needed some time to figure out what we were going to do next. I went to the lounge, got coffee, rolled my eyes at one of my teachers who had witnessed the event, and walked back into my office. By this time, DeAudra had stopped crying and I had cooled off and was ready to find out the great mystery of the stocking hat that couldn't be taken off.

"DeAudra, come on, do you really want to get a detention for this?"

"I ain't takin' it off—send me home," DeAudra said as she started to cry again.

"Fine, keep it on all day," I replied. "I guess I can let everyone keep their hats on all the time now, and then we can have fights in the hall because the boys will be running around pulling off hats, playing, acting like a bunch of idiots. But, okay, we will let everyone wear a hat all the time, DeAudra," I sarcastically preached.

"You white, you don't know, Mr. Anderson," DeAudra said, sighing and gasping. These noises were accompanied by a cry that only a 13-year-old girl with a broken heart can make.

"I've been called a racist before, DeAudra, and I don't like it," I shot back, trying to not get mad. I knew I had screwed up. There was something under that hat I didn't want to see. And that she didn't want anyone to see.

"I ain't called you a racist," she said, sobbing even harder.

How was I still making this worse? Was I really so stupid that I couldn't figure out why a little girl wouldn't take off a stocking cap?

"Fine, but you aren't going to class until you can tell me why you won't take that hat off," I pleaded.

The Kid in Purple Pants

Structured Approaches to Educating Underprivileged Students

We sat at an impasse for about 20 more minutes. Finally, DeAudra chimed, "I want to talk to Mrs. Clayton."

Yes! Why hadn't I thought of that a long time ago? Mrs. Shakeita Clayton was our school counselor and was the solution to my problem. I had finally realized that this was more than a discipline problem, it was a girl problem.

Mrs. Clayton reached my office in a flash. She smiled broadly at me and then turned her big smile toward DeAudra. She knew before DeAudra opened her mouth what had happened and why she was in the principal's office. I was asked to leave my office, and I will not lie, I did not have to be asked twice. Five short minutes later, the counselor emerged grinning and shaking her head at me.

"What?" I implored.

"Pat, you don't want her to take that hat off," Mrs. Clayton said with a smirk. Then she explained to me the sophisticated and unique world of African-American hair. I was dumbfounded. Shakeita, who is African American, knew everything there was to know about a little girl having a bad hair day. As a child, if I was having a bad hair day, I went and put my head under the sink and ran my fingers through my hair. Not the case for black girls.

"She should have told me that then," I said in my defense. "I would have let her keep it on and I wouldn't have yelled."

"Oh, okay, and then she would have been letting the whole school know that her hair was a mess," Mrs. Clayton replied. "She would rather fight with you then let those eighth-grade boys know that if they take off that hat, they are going to see a complete mess."

All I could do was apologize. I didn't understand and it was because I was white. DeAudra hadn't called me a racist after all. No, she had simply informed me that I was way out of touch with her needs and problems.

The Kid in Purple Pants

Structured Approaches to Educating Underprivileged Students

"You're going to have to let her wear the hat or send her home because that head of hair is not going to get fixed to-day," finished Shakeita with a smile and a pat on the back that said, *I know you're sorry.*

I went into the office and apologized to DeAudra while at the same time trying to save face by telling her that next time all she needed to do was tell me she needed to see me in private and I would understand and listen. What I was really saying was, "The next time I see a little girl with a hat on, I will ask to see them in private."

Did this situation make DeAudra different? Yes, DeAudra was put in a situation that caused her anxiety, fear, and anger because some middle-aged man knew nothing about what she was going through. Had her day been ruined? Did she learn one single thing that day? Was her mind focused on reducing a fraction to its lowest terms? Even if I had not done what I had, would her day have been okay? Was she scared when she walked into each classroom, anxious of what the teacher was going to do or say to her about that silly hat? Do you think she was scared of some goofy boy running by and pulling that hat off her head when she least expected it? Her day, even with-out my brilliant input, would have been filled with how to survive the day without becoming the subject of ridicule and embarrassment. Does this make her different than her best friend, Kayla?

Because she was poor, DeAudra's school experiences were completely unlike her friend Kayla's. Kayla was also African American, but her mom worked at Fashion Bug and got good discounts on nice clothes for her daughter. Plus, her father was a captain in the United States Air Force. When Kayla came to school, she felt good about herself. She would glow when we commented on how well she dressed and how pretty she looked each day. "I wish I had 48 pairs of shoes," I

The Kid in Purple Pants

Structured Approaches to Educating Underprivileged Students

said once as Kayla laughed and said I was crazy. Kayla's hair was always perfect, worn in a different style every couple of weeks.

This doesn't mean that Kayla, like all other children, doesn't have to cope with insecurity and self-consciousness. However, a poor kid has all those same insecurities that come with adolescence, compounded by problems brought about by poverty.

Educators must begin to focus on the different lines of attack available in instructing children living in poverty. The chore is much different and the social norms and stigmas associated with education influence those students and their desires and needs for schooling.

Job Equals Pride; Education Equals Burden

Poor kids are also different in that they often do not see the value of education. My two children understand the value of an education. My nieces and nephews understand it. My friends' children recognize it. Perhaps this is because they have all witnessed the benefits of education and what it enables an individual to do. My children know I love my job. They know I read books about school and speak to people about education. They have seen their aunts and uncles provide a good living for their children because of schooling. It is nothing foreign or new to them. These experiences are what make my children excited about their future and contemplating what will ultimately make them happy.

For a child coming from poverty, finding a job, any job, is better than being a burden. Searching the classified ads for whatever pays the most is what many poor people do to keep paying the bills. I distinctly remember my parents telling their five children, "Don't let the want ads determine what you will

The Kid in Purple Pants

Structured Approaches to Educating Underprivileged Students

do for a living." This struck a nerve in us all, as we understood what they meant. If we were to be truly happy, we could not rely on chance to give us a job that we cherish, and that makes us strive to become the best we possibly can become. But, even with the support of my parents, teachers, and older brothers, it was hard for me to visualize myself leaving behind a world of roofing and manual labor.

Discovering I was poor made a significant change in the person I was, the way I looked at the world, and how I felt about myself. My beliefs in what I was going to ultimately become when I was "all grown" started to change. I started to see a future I had never visualized before my grand discovery. Before then, you couldn't have told me that I could not be a teacher, doctor, or astronaut, if that is what I wanted. Miss Patrick had even told me in second grade that I was smart enough to be the president of the United States. By seventh grade, however, I just knew I would not be a teacher and that I was going to end up putting roofs on houses the rest of my life, going to bars after work, and marrying some girl with bad teeth, a loud mouth, and who was constantly mad at me because I spent my whole paycheck on Friday night. I didn't draw this conclusion by chance; I had seen this as the reality of many young men I grew to know during my adolescence. More than once, I experienced some of the guys working for my Dad pulling up to work on Monday morning and asking me for a few dollars so they could buy some cigarettes. At the same time, their girlfriends or wives yelled out the car window to borrow some money so they could get some diapers. I really did think this was my destiny, and I was seeing it reinforced every single day. Many of the men who came to work for my Dad were angry, hated school, and thought all their teachers had been stuck-up snobs who despised them. So even though my parents had told me repeatedly that I could do

The Kid in Purple Pants

Structured Approaches to Educating Underprivileged Students

whatever I wanted, this was the reality I saw. It was the picture that was being painted of what the sons of roofers become. How would I imagine anything different?

This is no different than the realities of many of my students. On more than one occasion I have been laughed at when I asked a former student if he or she were going to college after graduating high school. The responses I receive are heartbreaking. Some of the brightest students I have ever taught react to that question like it is the funniest joke they had ever heard. Their perception of what is possible for them has been skewed by what they have seen become the reality for everyone at their social status.

Would the picture being painted for me have been different if my father had been a doctor or lawyer? Would I have experienced conversations that were vastly different from those I heard on the rooftops? Of course. Sons and daughters of doctors become doctors. Sons and daughters of lawyers become lawyers. We know this is not always the case, but it does not take a genius to recognize that children often follow in the footsteps of their parents. The belief systems instilled in us as youngsters last in perpetuity. Why do we not note these differences when educating our youth?

Is it any wonder that many of our poor students do not see that they have the potential to utilize what they learn in school to make a living? The benefits of a quality education were not something often talked about on the roof. If education was discussed, it was to degrade it and talk about how it was for rich kids and stuck-up brats who were too lazy to work hard for a living.

Of all the conversations I have ever had on top of a roof, none compares to my conversation with my brother Kyle about the virtues of Niccolo Machiavelli's book *The Prince*. We were both reading *The Prince* and had some distinct and

The Kid in Purple Pants

Structured Approaches to Educating Underprivileged Students

strong opinions about the merits, morality, and overall usefulness it might possess in being a leader. Now, let me say that the conversation became heated as we both stuck to our guns on what we believed and our own take on what exactly Machiavelli was trying to impart. Our voices got louder, and we actually put down our tear-off tools and stopped working, all to better make our points. I defended the fact that as a leader sometimes it was necessary to be merciless and make decisions for others that might be in the best interest of the society as a whole while unfortunately, at the same time, taking liberties with some individual human rights. Kyle, however, did not find value in my argument. He saw Machiavelli as a nutcase who, if he had actually ever been a real leader, would have been overthrown and killed because he was cruel and would never be considered a legitimate ruler to his people.

Suffice it to say that this was not considered a typical conversation that takes place between roofers while doing hard labor. We began to draw the attention of everyone else working with us that day. As our argument reached another climax, the distinctively deep and raspy voice of Mike, a longtime roofer and family friend, called to my father, who was working on the other side of the roof. "Hey, Harry, why didn't you tell us your boys were fags?" This question startled us from our passionate discourse as everyone on the roof roared with laughter and wholeheartedly agreed with Mike and his perception of the two of us. In Mike's opinion, as well as everyone else's on the roof that day, a heated conversation about a philosophical book written in the 16th century made my brother and me less manly than the rest of them. Making a crude comment about our sexuality was Mike's way of telling us that talking about books and arguing over something written almost 500 years ago in his opinion was fairly stupid. He soon concluded his assessment by informing us both that, be-

The Kid in Purple Pants

Structured Approaches to Educating Underprivileged Students

cause of our argument over a stupid book, we hadn't even noticed that a very pretty woman was now swimming in the pool two doors down and we had a perfect view from the roof.

Why tell the Machiavelli story? It is just one more example of what many poor students experience as truth as it relates to the intrinsic worth of education. What Mike felt would be an insult to our manhood is, for many young people, the mind frame they experience, which is fostered by the lack of value many poor people find in education. Many young people are not as lucky as I am and fall victim to this mindset and even perpetuate the belief to their children, which only escalates and continues the endless cycle of the self-fulfilling prophecy that nothing can or will ever change.

I have had countless conversations with fellow roofers about horrific school experiences that include being hit in the back of the head, choked, and called endless degrading names and being ridiculed for such a minor infraction as having dirty fingernails. These thoughts, experiences, and ideas become ingrained in our poor students and become the focus of what they see as veracity and the only means of making a living while trying to sustain a little self-respect. Everyone wants to feel like they belong to something. And a club of guys who hate school, work hard, and also play hard is not a bad group to belong to if you can find it.

It's hard to fathom, but when you are poor, there are benefits to quitting school and getting a job. It sounds nuts, I know, but there is a lot of truth in it. A job will get you things that you would never otherwise obtain. Employment gives you worth and respect, whereas going to school is considered a burden on the family. Going to school requires new clothes and shoes, as well as money for supplies. But if you hold down a job, you are a provider who can help ease the pain of being in financial hardship. And that is a nice feeling, know-

The Kid in Purple Pants

Structured Approaches to Educating Underprivileged Students

ve contributed to the betterment of your family.
on is strong and very difficult to overcome when
young adolescent who is helping your family meet
needs. There was no greater feeling than to know I
to help provide for my family. The appreciation and
admiration I obtained was rewarding. My father knew he had
someone who could be counted on to do what was needed
when it was crunch time. He didn't hide the fact that he knew
this and confided in me about what needed to be accomplished. It made a 19-year-old boy feel like a man.

Guilt, Belonging, and Knowing the Score

While attending college and doing what I really wanted to do
(studying literature), I felt, in a lot of ways, that I was a burden to my family. I was not working or producing anything. I
felt guilty many times as I sat around on a Saturday morning
watching cartoons with my roommates. I experienced shame
that while I was sleeping off a hangover, I knew my Dad and
little brother would be waking at 5:30 a.m. to work to make
money that would help me pay for school. One's sense of
duty to the family becomes very strong when each member is
united in working for a common goal—survival.

The guilt associated with bettering one's self is genuine
and can influence a person to knowingly do things not in his
best interest. Enabling students to get past this is difficult and
requires a concerted effort. Educators must also note that this
thought process is not observable, thus making it almost impossible to detect and alter. It means that counselors and
teachers have to almost be mind readers in order to intervene.

It wasn't like roofing was a bad gig. Some of the greatest
days of my life have been spent on a roof. Some of my funni-

The Kid in Purple Pants

Structured Approaches to Educating Underprivileged Students

est moments and most heartfelt laughs have also been experienced while dirty, tired, and roof-bound.

I distinctly remember one summer when all the guys who worked for my Dad were collecting Marlboro Points, which were little proofs of purchase tabs that a smoker would tear off the cigarette package to redeem for merchandise. My younger brother and I never smoked, but everyone else on the crew did.

One scorching day Dave exclaimed with excitement, while lighting up a cigarette, "I got enough points to get two sleeping bags and a T-shirt."

My brother thought this was hilarious and said, "That's nothing, Mike has enough to buy a Marlboro jet plane." Mike was a heavy smoker, and his deep smoker's voice only made what he said even more hilarious as he barked, "Bro, you ain't kiddin.'"

Upon hearing this, Kyle yelled, "Only problem is, the air is too thin up there for him to go for a ride in it."

We all cackled, and Mike chimed in once again, "Bro, you ain't kiddin.'"

I would not trade those hot summer memories for anything in the world. I loved the guys I worked with and believed they would do anything for me. They respected that I worked hard and put forth just as much effort as they did. I was part of something that was doing some good. We had pride. And sometimes, when you are poor, that's all you have. We were proud that we could do something that not many people could do. We would rise at 5:00 a.m. and work nonstop until 8:00 p.m. I cherished the times that a happy homeowner would come out and see what we were able to accomplish in a relatively short amount of time. "Wow, I would have never thought you could do that much work in this kind of heat," was something I loved to hear. It was a sense of

The Kid in Purple Pants

Structured Approaches to Educating Underprivileged Students

pride and we would work hard, not just for the paycheck, but for the notoriety as well. It gave us value and self-worth.

It should be easy to see that underprivileged kids might find consolation in this type of work atmosphere and make it their life goal. Is that bad? No, but it does answer a few questions on why it might be difficult for teachers to overcome the challenges that face them when it comes to shifting the mind frames of students in these surroundings. This is why providing social equity to poor students is vital in the educational experience.

My own children are probably the two most naïve kids ever to walk the face of the planet. They are smart as whips, but fortunately they have limited knowledge of how the real world works. I would not want it any other way, because that would mean I would not be in the type of financial situation that affords them this luxury.

Last summer my daughter, Taylor, went on a seven-day trip to New York with her school band. She was so excited. She saw a Broadway show, the Empire State Building, and a host of other New York landmarks. I was thrilled for her. I have never been any farther east than Indianapolis, and the idea of my daughter experiencing the Big Apple was exhilarating. The trip cost around $1,500 plus spending money, which is not a bad deal for such a trip. The school allowed students to pay the fee in installments. When one of Taylor's $150 installments was due, she simply walked up to me and, in her sweet, innocent 14-year-old voice, declared, "Dad, I need a check for $150 tomorrow morning." Now, don't get me wrong, $150 is not a lot of money for me. But the idea that Taylor had no qualms about asking for that amount of money, that she had no fear of rejection, was a little too much for me. I realized that my daughter doesn't really know the value of money. She truly believes that you simply obtain money from

The Kid in Purple Pants

Structured Approaches to Educating Underprivileged Students

your parents so you can buy stuff. That creates a lot of fear in me.

I have experienced the same thing with my 10-year-old son, Scott. I am flabbergasted when he says such gems as, "I can't stand it when Becky [the house cleaner] comes. She always puts my stuff where I can't find it." The first time I heard those words uttered from his mouth I practically went into cardiac arrest. Did my son really just say that he can't stand it when a lady comes into our home, cleans it, picks up his toys, changes his sheets, and even thanks us for allowing her to do so? It was beyond my comprehension.

But I have to ask myself whether he is to blame for thinking that way. The answer is no. And neither is Taylor for not knowing the value of a dollar. They are upper middle-class children whose parents (mostly me) never wanted them to know what it is like to not have whatever it was their hearts desired.

On the other hand, I understood at age 14 everything there was to realize about money and how it worked. I was not naïve. I knew how to rip the numbers off the bottom of a check so we would have a few extra days to get the money in the bank before it was processed. I understood what "float time" meant when writing a check on a Saturday and having until 3:00 p.m. on a Tuesday before it would be processed at the bank. I knew that a $15 service charge was going to be charged for a bad check, but it was better than not having dinner that night. Naïve? No. Different? Yes! I would have never asked my parents for the money to go on a $1,500 trip to New York. I wouldn't have wanted to embarrass them. I wouldn't have wanted them to have to tell me that they couldn't afford it. And I certainly wouldn't have wanted them to work extra hard to get me there.

The Kid in Purple Pants

Structured Approaches to Educating Underprivileged Students

I remember my father vomiting from heat exhaustion and writhing in pain from cramping due to dehydration. He was working in 95-degree weather trying to finish a small roof that he and I were doing alone so we could cash out the job and have enough money to pay off my little brother's elementary school tuition so he would be allowed to attend his graduation ceremony that evening. Asking for money to go to New York to see some Broadway show and the Empire State Building was, in my poverty state of mind, greedy and something only a spoiled brat would even want. The mind structure that comes with living in poverty creates resentment for the finer things in life. It causes so much resentment that it makes someone not aspire for such things because they seem so un-attainable. If poor students feel this way about the better things in life, what makes them want to work hard and devote extra time to difficult tasks that seem useless if the work is never going to materialize into something tangible?

I Dislike Cops

When you are poor, it's hard to trust people. I hated cops more than anything in the entire world when I was a kid. I have to admit that I still don't care for policemen. I don't know why that is, but I do. I don't have anything to hide. I don't speed...much. I am about as dorky as they come. I have taught my kids to be respectful of the law and that police officers are their friend and that they're here to help, but I still get a nervousness in my stomach every time I see the police. If I am on the highway and going the speed limit, I get nauseous, my mind starts to whirl, and I try to think of all the reasons why the cop next to me might pull me over. If I am waiting in line at a fast food restaurant and a police officer walks through the doors, I cringe and try not to make eye contact. I

The Kid in Purple Pants

Structured Approaches to Educating Underprivileged Students

am 40 years old and I am not able to overcome the fact that I am no longer breaking the law every time I sit down behind the wheel of an automobile. I suppose I still envision my brothers, with ladders sticking out beyond the legal limit of the bed of a dinged pickup, screaming expletives because they were worried they were going to get pulled over the second they saw a cop car. Or, I see myself as an 18-year-old, cursing and nervous behind the wheel of a dump truck, hoping that the cop who just pulled behind me doesn't see that my license plate is expired or hear that the muffler is too loud and notice that it is being held up by a hanger I had wrapped around it to keep it from falling off.

Getting your truck impounded or, even worse, getting arrested, can send the family into turmoil. An impounded truck means you can't get to work the next day, you don't get paid, and you now have no way of getting your truck back. Getting arrested does the same thing. I, along with many of my students, have seen this happen. It is emotionally and financially draining on a child and causes misguided trust issues to form and exist for a very long time.

I know that many of my students feel the same way about me as I did about the police. They see me as an authority figure and don't want to cross my path for anything in the world. They don't trust me any more than I trust a cop.

Despite being a feared authority figure, I am a "hugger." I hug my students, tousle their hair, tease them about boyfriends and girlfriends, and try to make a connection with each of them. I ask them questions about their weekends, how their parents are doing, and how older siblings are faring at the local high school. I want them to know I genuinely care about them. But, I discern that for many of my students these encounters with me provoke dread and anxiety. I understand that the principal is not the most well-liked guy in the school

The Kid in Purple Pants

Structured Approaches to Educating Underprivileged Students

and students do not, as a rule, flock to the principal to have deep, heartfelt conversations. But this goes beyond that. Some of my poor students avoid eye contact with me when I see them in the halls or are quick to answer with an "okay" or "nothing" response to an inquiry I may have posed. And I know it's because they are hiding something. They are trying to conceal the fact that they may not be living in the school district any longer and have been warned that they better not say anything or they may be forced to change schools. The sight of the person who is supposed to make certain they are getting a good education is actually causing them unease and may be adversely affecting their ability to learn. They also know that they do not have any lunch money on their account, are embarrassed, and don't want to "have to talk to Mr. Anderson" about getting it paid off. Or, probably the worst situation of all, they are afraid to tell me about their older brother or sister who might have dropped out of school and is not doing well. It is embarrassing to admit that your sister—the one Mr. Anderson said was the "best persuasive essay writer" in the entire eighth grade—has dropped out of school. It's nothing to be proud of and certainly enough to make one want to divert eye contact and finish the day hassle free.

How to Build Trust with Untrusting Students:

> * Allow students the benefit of the doubt sometimes; students who feel as though they are trusted will trust you.
>
> * Share some of your own concerns for the class (not student concerns). Asking your students' opinions and for input helps them feel like you trust their ideas.

The Kid in Purple Pants

Structured Approaches to Educating Underprivileged Students

> * Talk about yourself, your family, and your interests: Show students you are a person, not just someone who gives homework or runs school assemblies.
>
> * Assign important classroom tasks to students and explain the significance of the task to you. When the students understand that you are trusting them with something imperative, they will know you trust them.
>
> * Make eye contact and be an active listener. Don't interrupt.
>
> * Empathize and remember what it was like to be 11, 14, or 17 years old. Don't minimize a student's problem. Avoid the temptation of saying things like, "Oh, that's nothing to worry about, you will have bigger problems than that when you get older." These types of comments show students how out of touch you are with them. Trust comes from understanding.

Need That Connection

Teachers must also make a conscious effort to build positive relationships with students that go above and beyond what is needed by the ordinary student. This means an approach to loving children who need it while at the same time maintaining a relationship that fosters respect and a desire to prosper and succeed.

I often reflect on the philosophy of a young second-year teacher who stated, in no compromising terms, "I like to treat my students like my little cousins. I show them I love them and respect them, but make sure they also know that I mean

The Kid in Purple Pants

Structured Approaches to Educating Underprivileged Students

business." When I heard these words I realized this was an approach to teaching that fosters love, kindness, and support, but most important (especially in the case of underprivileged students), a no-nonsense approach to learning and the importance respect plays in a school environment. This young teacher had already figured out that teaching was not simply about ensuring that students were ready for test day, but that the only way to prepare students for life was to give them the opportunity to be successful in an environment that not only fostered love, but also encouraged a sense of respect and self-worth. "I mean business" is the perfect way of letting a child know that, "I love you, but I am also going to push you to be successful."

As I said earlier, the word "different" isn't the best way to describe poor kids. Because poor kids are no different when it comes to what they want and how they want to be treated. The desire to be happy, popular, accepted, and loved is the same for everyone, no matter one's economic situation.

The last thing I ever wanted to be was different. I wanted to have two pairs of blue jeans, a nice car to take a girl on a date in, and a sense of self-worth to allow me the confidence to not care about the jeans or the car. Underprivileged children simply come to school with values and ideas that are not conducive to success in our present education system. And if we continue to ignore that underprivileged children need resources that others may not, we will continue to miss opportunities to better educate all our children and enhance their education to give them the opportunity to succeed and live the lives they choose.

The Kid in Purple Pants

Structured Approaches to Educating Underprivileged Students

My Favorite Trust Quotes:

"One of the best things I ever did as a principal was allowing students to retrieve things from my car for me, go into my office without me there, watch a class for me [junior high boys helping to monitor first-grade recess]. Once these kids knew I trusted them not to steal from me, knew I knew they could be counted on, and knew I loved them, they had my back. These were students that now, instead of fighting or vandalizing, were helping to stop student fights and vandalism for me. I showed them I trusted them; it wasn't something they had experienced before. They liked it. I loved it."

Steve Amizich

"Once they trust me, they don't want to disappoint me."

Gina James

"If you didn't trust someone, would you really tell them that your electricity is turned off, you didn't have supper last night, and you don't have any idea where you are going to sleep that night? I know I wouldn't. A kid has to trust you if you are going to find out what makes him tick."

Ed Graves

The Kid in Purple Pants

Structured Approaches to Educating Underprivileged Students

Poverty must not be a bar to learning
and learning must offer an escape
from poverty.

Lyndon B. Johnson

The Kid in Purple Pants

Structured Approaches to Educating Underprivileged Students

Chapter 4

Maslow's Hierarchy of Needs: Not Just for College Freshmen Anymore

I believe that, as long as there is plenty, poverty is evil."

—Robert Kennedy

The class I remember most as a college freshman was my first psychology course. That class taught me about what makes us tick. In other words, we contemplated why we do the things we do and why our parents drive us crazy. And, of course, we pondered the age-old question: If a tree falls in the woods and no one is there to hear it, does it make a sound? Many of my college roommates became psychology majors after their first semester in college because of that class. Learning about Sigmund Freud and Ivan Pavlov was very enlightening. To be sure, Freud and Pavlov's research and theories sparked many interesting discussions among my roommates and me, but I much preferred to study Maslow's theories on how an individual can possibly ever become self-actualized.

In that class, I learned about Maslow's whole "hierarchy of needs" for the very first time. Was my professor saying that if I didn't have enough food to eat, I wasn't ever going to be able to finish college? Was this Maslow guy really thinking that I had to feel "secure" and "wanted" in order to have any

| The Kid in Purple Pants |

Structured Approaches to Educating Underprivileged Students

real deep thoughts that could one day change the world? I couldn't understand this. I knew a ton of people, myself included, who were not living in suitable homes, and sure as hell didn't feel secure about anything, especially money. As I sat and listened to the professor explain the varied levels that eventually are supposed to lead to self-actualization, I just knew this Maslow guy must be off his rocker. How could anyone feel that way about everything in this stupid pyramid? I mean, the love stuff I understood. I could get as much love and laughter as I needed by simply calling home. My Dad and little brother could always provide me with laughter. And if I told my Mom that one of my classes was "really" hard, she would tell me how smart I was and that I should not give up and keep trying and thus I would get my love fix in.

For those of us who might have been able to get through life without having to learn about Maslow, or for those who might need a refresher, this is for you. Maslow's theory was that an individual—to be truly happy (i.e., self-actualized) and able to fully appreciate his surroundings—must first meet a hierarchy of basic needs. Those basic needs, which Maslow arranged on a pyramid, start with physiological requirements such as food and water. Going up the pyramid, safety is the next basic need and consists of security of resources, body, family, and health. Love/belonging and esteem are the next two needs that all humans must have met if they wish to climb the pyramid toward becoming self-actualized. Obtaining friendships, family relationships, respect from others, and achievement are vital needs that must be met. And finally, at the top of the pyramid, is self-actualization. A self-actualized person theoretically has the capability to problem solve, be creative, and have a total lack of prejudice. Seems simple enough, right? Yet, for many of the students we are teaching,

The Kid in Purple Pants

Structured Approaches to Educating Underprivileged Students

making their way up this pyramid to becoming critical thinkers and creative young people is nearly impossible.

Food

Many of our students do not have the most basic needs of food and shelter met. They come to school hungry, simply thinking of how to get something to eat while simultaneously not wanting anyone to know how truly hungry they really are. I have witnessed poor students making a joke of eating from a fellow student's plate. I have seen students going from one student to the next, asking is there is anything that isn't going to be eaten. I once disciplined a student for stealing a treat from a teacher's desk, only to find out later that the kid was hungry, had no lunch money, and had been brought to school too late for breakfast. He felt he had no choice. I have witnessed hunger, and it is one of the saddest things any individual should ever have to endure or experience. Our children *must* have their basic needs met, especially if we can provide it to them with very little effort.

The National School Lunch Program is a wonderful thing. Established in 1946 during the Truman administration, it's a federally assisted meal program that operates for all children in public and non-profit private schools. Today, more than 31 million students are served each school day. Unlike many programs funded by the government, this one is well-supported and has not put any additional burden on local school resources. Along with the free breakfast program, educators are now able to provide students with two decent meals a day before they are sent home to fend for themselves for their third.

Unfortunately, many families are eligible for these benefits but do not take advantage. Often the reason is simple:

The Kid in Purple Pants

Structured Approaches to Educating Underprivileged Students

pride. We all have pride, and that is not necessarily a bad thing. Having pride in a job well done is respectable and admirable. We all can appreciate someone who will not stop until he has accomplished a goal. But, being prideful to the point that it hurts children is not good. Throughout my career, I have known many parents who would not participate in the program for the simple fact that they, as children, participated in the program and were subject to ridicule and embarrassment.

Although I attended a private parochial school, we were still eligible for free lunches and could participate in the program by walking from St. Bernard's to the public school across the street. Why my family never participated, I will never know. We were eligible, and I know we could have benefited from not having to worry about the added expense of feeding five kids lunch each day. And, trust me, it was a burden. I remember many times waking up and looking for change anywhere we could find it, or going to school and telling my teacher I had forgotten my lunch money at home and that I would bring it in the next day. We ate school lunch because it was cheaper than having to pack lunches for five children. I suppose it was pride that kept my parents from utilizing the program or the same reason we attended private school when we could not afford it. It was their attempt at sheltering their children from the cruelties of the world of poverty and at the same time enabling them to experience self-confidence and an environment where education was a priority.

I don't remember many students from St. Bernard's being free or reduced-lunch children, but there were at least a few. They were embarrassed and did not like being free lunch children.

The Kid in Purple Pants

Structured Approaches to Educating Underprivileged Students

There was usually a fairly long line of students waiting for hot lunch when we arrived at the back entrance of the public school, Lewis and Clark Elementary. As we lined up, the lunch ladies would make the free and reduced-lunch kids go to the front of the line and get their lunches first. As a child, I never understood why this was necessary, but do recall that it was the source of much embarrassment. "Why does he get to go to the front of the line? That's bull!" was screamed out more than once as the less-fortunate children were paraded to the front of the line. Cutting in line is one of the all-time worse things a student can do in elementary school, so when it was pointed out, everyone looked and listened with extreme attention and annoyance.

To make a bad situation worse, the lunch monitor would quietly, because she thought she was doing the right thing, walk to the accuser and whisper into his ear the reason why that particular student was able to go to the front of the line, no questions asked. I remember thinking that I would rather starve and die a horrible death than go to the front of the line. The lunch tickets even had "F/R" written on the back with either the "F" or "R" circled to indicate free or reduced price. I suppose this process of making the free lunch kids go first was so that the ladies could easily keep track of paid and free lunches and keep things in better order. But, the embarrassment was still there.

We have all known someone (if not ourselves) who was a "free lunch" kid. We all remember that awkwardness of looking at our lunch tickets and seeing they were different than those of our friends. It was something we didn't talk about, but it was there and real in the mind of that student who had a different ticket. It is no wonder that it is very difficult for parents to subject their children to those same experiences.

The Kid in Purple Pants

Structured Approaches to Educating Underprivileged Students

Statistics show—even in schools with very high poverty levels—that more than 35% of families who qualify for breakfast and lunch assistance go without help. The reasons are either the lack of education or apathetic school systems that do not actively engage families that may be in need of assistance. School systems are allowing families to miss opportunities to meet the fundamental needs of their children. When this occurs, those missing components reflect in students with poor behavior, anger, frustration, and both physical and psychological problems. The time and effort it takes to remedy these problems are miniscule when compared to the positive results they will ultimately have on the lives of students and their ability to learn.

School systems must mandate that everyone complete a School Lunch Program application. When each parent is required to fill out the application, the stigma attached disappears and parents are free to submit an application without fear of feeling as though they are trying to receive a handout.

I have witnessed a single mother or working poor parents try to secretly fill out applications during school registration nights out of fear someone would find out they were having financial problems. The shame must stop. Our present environment and approach to helping poor students breed shame and resentment. Why make anyone suffer any ridicule if this can easily be taken care of by simply having *all* parents fill out the same paperwork? The burden of completing each of these applications is minimal when compared with the positive impact it brings to the lives of many students who are living in homes where finances are a problem.

The Kid in Purple Pants

Structured Approaches to Educating Underprivileged Students

Mentors

Not many students are as lucky as I was when it comes to having mentors. I didn't have a mentor come to my school once a week and shoot baskets with me or play a board game like many of my students. Instead, I had older brothers that I respected and idolized because they were my protectors and showed me right from wrong (well, *almost* always showed me right from wrong). They were not perfect, but they were very good at showing me what I needed to do to be successful and maintain my self-worth. They gave me a road map on how to conduct myself in school, how to treat people less fortunate than myself, and how to defend myself against anyone who ever tried to hurt or intimidate me. Not bad for two poor kids who were only trying to look out for each other and their little brothers and sister.

But, like I said, not all students are fortunate enough to have what I had. This is why the development of mentor programs can play an important role in giving students an opportunity to see how life is on the other side. "Life on the other side," what does that mean? It means that when students are mentored by a retired air force captain, or schoolteacher, or small business owner, they are seeing, many times over, what life is like OUTSIDE of poverty. Mentors provide a glimpse of what life can be like outside of what a student seems as the norm. It gives a student an opportunity to build a relationship with someone who has experienced many different things that the child has never experienced or has even known anyone to experience. Giving some of my students the opportunity to speak with members of the U.S. Air Force and have conversations about the vast places and things they have seen and done during their careers has been eye-opening for many students. I have spoken with students who, in great detail, can now de-

The Kid in Purple Pants

Structured Approaches to Educating Underprivileged Students

scribe what life is like as an investment banker, author, fighter pilot, and police officer. It is an experience that can never be taken away.

A mentor willing to come into our schools, spend an hour a week with a child he or she doesn't know, and provide guidance and support to one of our students is the kind of person we want to associate with. We want them to see what life is like for our most needy children. The community relationships built will pay large dividends to our schools. They are the voice to the community that says we are doing the right things for children. They will be the first ones to help with passing referendums and providing local business support to our schools, and they are always first in line to help at any school function. If we provide our community members with a way to help and assist us, they will rise to the challenge and be our strongest advocates.

Outreach

Making resources available to those in need is vital if the basic needs of all our children are to be met. We must make a commitment to maintaining our social workers and counselors and training them to understand the needs of our families. The effort must come from the district, not the parents. If we wait for the parents to ask for help, it may come too late and not truly benefit the child. Why would we want to linger until things are so horrible for parents that they must ask for assistance? Go in search of these people. Mandate that counselors, principals, and teachers work registration nights and be invasive. Pry and dig for information. Man your registration nights, parent/teacher evenings, school dances, and social functions like a police officer on a stakeout. Train teachers to ask questions and find out what is going on in the homes of their students. It is the only way to uncover what is taking place at home. It is also a great opportunity to create a relationship with a parent that enables a teacher to better connect academically with students.

Many parents do not feel comfortable talking with administrators about needing assistance. Remember, authority figures can be intimidating and be cause to not attend school functions and parent/teacher conferences. If the basic needs of your students are to be met, teachers must help in this endeavor and understand that it is a responsibility of theirs to go in search of those who need the extra assistance. With the proper training and reinforcement, they will quickly understand the importance and work hard to shed some light on what is going on in the homes of some of our most needy children.

I have made home visits to trailers that should have been condemned. Some of the living conditions our students are faced with are almost unbearable. On one occasion I was delivering a gas card to a parent living in a trailer that was less than six feet wide. It was more of a camping-style trailer that had been placed on blocks, but it was acting as the sole means of shelter for this family. I was taking the card to the parent because she had recently become homeless and was living in this trailer that sat about 12 miles from our school district boundaries. This woman's daughter with special needs was making remarkable strides. She had a wonderful teacher who cared for her and loved her in every way. Her teacher understood her needs and had dedicated herself to making certain that Heather was getting exactly what she needed to be successful. Heather's mother was considered homeless, so we had been able to provide her with some monetary help in getting her daughter to school. This mother had committed herself to providing a ride for her child each morning even

The Kid in Purple Pants

Structured Approaches to Educating Underprivileged Students

though simply placing her on a bus in the new school district would have been much simpler and affordable. But she had made the decision to do what she thought was right for her little girl's education. She would drive the 12 miles each morning to our district because, as she explained, "I know you love her here and take care of her. I don't trust anyone else to care for her." Although she needed some financial assistance, she was able to provide for her daughter the education that she knew was best. She showed commitment and dedication to her daughter that I have not seen in many parents who have been in a much better situation. This mother still was able to maintain her automobile and got her daughter to school on time, clean, and ready to learn every day. No easy task for a woman living in a home many of us have parked in our backyards waiting to be used for our one or two camping excursions a year.

Changing the Stigma

The unmerited stigma that is sometimes placed on poor parents must also end. Because these parents sometimes make poor decisions and are not the best at budgeting money or utilizing resources the way they should, teachers and administrators sometimes pass them off as not caring or being apathetic when it comes to caring for their children. This is not the case and is simply a cultural and generational poverty problem that is nearly impossible to overcome without proper interventions.

How do I know this stigma exists? It existed for my family. On more than one occasion I have been approached by acquaintances from my childhood. For the most part the conversations are quick and painless. However, there are those that become awkward. I have been asked what I do for a liv-

The Kid in Purple Pants

Structured Approaches to Educating Underprivileged Students

74

ing and what my siblings are up to now. The utter shock and surprise in their faces and voices is proof enough that the last thing they ever expected from an Anderson kid was that he or she was going to grow up and be successful. "Harry is a lawyer? Michael is a geologist?" These are the things I hear as they look at me puzzled and confused as to how this could have possibly happened. These stigmas exist and sometimes play into the way teachers might interact with a student who they feel has no future other than what they might stumble upon.

I recently spoke to a large group of superintendents at a county administrator meeting. I have spoken to large groups of people in the past and I enjoyed it immensely. There is nothing I like better than sharing what I have learned with others. But I knew this speaking engagement was going to be different. I was nervous to speak about the benefits of accurately accounting for the number of homeless students residing within St. Clair County. Why would I be nervous to talk to these men and women about something I feel so passionate and care so deeply about? Why would I be apprehensive to give tips on how to make certain that students are getting what they need? Or explain in detail how to better meet the needs of the most disadvantaged students we have in our schools? I was nervous because many of these administrators have a philosophical objection to the laws that mandate schools must give extra support to those students who are homeless.

In Illinois, the McKinney-Vento Act is very controversial. Many administrators feel it adds an unfair burden onto school systems because it mandates that the district pay transportation and supply costs and a host of other benefits for homeless students. The mindset of many school leaders is that these students are not truly homeless because they may be residing with other family members, are living in hotels, or living in a

The Kid in Purple Pants

Structured Approaches to Educating Underprivileged Students

shelter. They feel that homeless students are only homeless if they are living on the streets or in automobiles. These local school leaders have witnessed people taking advantage of the system and have grown callous to the needs of those who are not in need but simply abusing the system. What is not understood is that these unfortunate examples of abuse are not the rule, but the exception, and are what keeps us from helping those most in need. The glaring examples of abusing the system are outshining the different ways in which we have helped better the lives of those who are in great need. It is another example of the middle-class mind frame at work. The resentment for what these administrators feel about those taking advantage is causing many in St. Clair County to have to do without. The resources are not being distributed to the county because there does not seem to be a need. However, this is the same county that houses East St. Louis. Although many positive changes are presently taking place in East St. Louis with state help and guidance, the attention given to homeless students must be stepped up. Educators can blame no one but themselves for not making it clear to those in power what conditions are like in the trenches. If we do not provide a road map to our elected officials, how will they know what road to take in helping to reform and support our schools? They can't, and they won't.

This holds true for not only administrators, but for many teachers as well. I have witnessed many angry, upset, and frustrated teachers, myself included, who feel passionately about not allowing for the abuse of money and support for the poor students, who are supposed to be provided for with this money. I have seen teachers stating that these "homeless" kids are wearing nicer clothes and using better cell phones than the teachers themselves are wearing and using.

The Kid in Purple Pants

Structured Approaches to Educating Underprivileged Students

I understand the frustration and share in it when I witness such abuse. However, we cannot afford for these exceptions to the rule to keep us from fighting for those parents and students who are not abusing the system. Teachers and administrators are the only advocates that poor students have, and if funding and support is to continue, we cannot allow for abusers of these benefits to keep those in need from acquiring them. We must provide professional development that teaches educators these benefits so that they understand the needs and benefits that the additional resources will provide.

In St. Clair County, I estimate that more than 70% of students eligible for homeless benefits are not receiving them because they have not been identified. The problem of underreporting has been devastating. As the economy has worsened, the number of children living in poverty in America has risen to 1 in 6. In St. Clair County, records indicate this number is closer to 1 in 4. With almost 25% of our students living in poverty, why would anyone not want to properly report the homeless population within one's district? Along with the philosophical differences, many find it unappealing to openly admit they have a large population of at-risk students attending their school. Although no one paints a sign on the side of the building stating this fact, many feel it may give the district a reputation for having difficult students, discipline problems, and crime.

On more than one occasion, I have had a teacher come to me after meeting with a parent and explain a bad financial situation, or even worse, a drug problem. I distinctly remember one instance, after a very concerning parent/teacher conference, a particular teacher came to me and said she was pretty sure that she'd had a conference with a parent under the influence of drugs. The parent could not keep her eyes open and was talking in slurred nonsense throughout the confer-

The Kid in Purple Pants

Structured Approaches to Educating Underprivileged Students

77

ence. We already had suspicions of drug abuse based on interviews with the student and our prior relationship with the parents. These same parents had been very responsible, attentive, and supportive only three years prior. Because the teacher had already been picking up on strange behaviors in the classroom, been attentive during the conference, and had the proper professional development to notice these behaviors, we were able to intervene and make a difference in that student's life and his family.

As I mentioned earlier, Maslow stressed that security and a safe haven are essential for all humans to function at high levels of intelligence. In order to feel safe and secure, educators must also realize that parents need to feel this exact same way. School must be a safe place to go if parents are going to want to go to school for things such as parent/teacher conferences. By safe, I simply mean that they must feel as though they will not be barraged with the difficulties they are already facing in the world.

We had a very bad practice at my current district. During parent/teacher conferences we would issue a bill for any unpaid library fines, lunch account charges, unpaid bus passes, and so on. At the time, it seemed like a great idea. What better way of collecting some unpaid debts than to get it while parents were in school getting ready to talk with a teacher?

Our middle-class mind frames were at work again. After all, I would appreciate knowing that if my son had lost a library book or had forgotten lunch money, I could reach into my wallet and make good on what he owed. It would clear one more thing off my plate and I would actually go home feeling good that I didn't have to worry about owing anyone money. It was this mentality that thought doing this with people who were poor was a good idea. Basically, each time a parent having any difficulty with money would walk through

The Kid in Purple Pants

Structured Approaches to Educating Underprivileged Students

the doors of our school to talk with a teacher about his/her child's academic progress, we would approach them with bills and financial burdens. There is nothing like being told by a teacher that you owe $18 in lunch charges and that your son still hasn't paid his bus fee while at the same time trying to figure out why he is earning an F in Reading. This is not what we should be doing. We cannot endure parents not wanting to come to school. We must make an attempt to make these meetings and school functions hassle-free and pleasurable. We learned that trying to collect back debts is the number one way of running parents out of a building feeling resentful and frustrated.

Research has proved that schools that make a conscious effort to become more inviting have seen increased attendance numbers, increases in parent volunteers, and better attendance to parent/teacher conferences and special education meetings.

Approaches to meeting the needs of those students and families that are lacking some of the basic needs are important and must not be overlooked or left to chance. Methodically, these approaches must be calculated, tested, and studied for effectiveness. Establishing leadership teams, parent volunteer clubs, and "counselor councils" goes a long way in helping to maintain an initiative that will thrive only if ownership to the effort is established quickly. Stewarding these programs is no easy task, and trying to go it alone is a disaster waiting to happen. Although it seems odd to spend so much time, re-sources, and energy on programs that deal almost entirely with simply preparing students to learn, we have no choice. We have tried things the other way and learned that it doesn't work. We have tried the "tough love" approach that simply produced failing students who couldn't contain themselves properly in a classroom environment. We did not actively pursue the help and support of our community and parents.

The Kid in Purple Pants

Structured Approaches to Educating Underprivileged Students

We thought we could do it alone and were theoretically doing a pretty good job of it. But, was it what we really wanted to do? We were essentially telling our parents that we didn't need them and that they were not needed in helping to educate and care for their children. We made them feel like outsiders; thus making them exactly that.

I think Maslow would be proud to know that his hierarchy of needs has been put to good use. The idea is basic. Provide a human being with the basic needs to function and, who knows, one day that person might actually figure out what it means to be "self-actualized."

The Kid in Purple Pants

Structured Approaches to Educating Underprivileged Students

Chapter 5

Knowing What They Need: Social Emotional Learning and Character Education

"The function of education is to teach one to think intensively and to think critically. Intelligence plus character—that is the goal of true education."

—Martin Luther King, Jr.

Social Emotional Learning:

On more than one occasion a fellow administrator has said to me, "Anderson, do you even teach reading or math in that school of yours anymore?" And my reply is, "Only after we have them ready to learn reading and math."

Of all the initiatives I have implemented in my school, social and emotional learning (SEL) has to be the most controversial and least understood. The constant barrage of criticism that comes with teaching students to be emotionally stable is mind-boggling for me. I don't understand how critics believe that teaching students the tools they need to be socially competent and emotionally stable is detrimental. How do educators fail to see the benefit of teaching students coping skills, stress management techniques, and conflict resolution aptitude? By simply affording the time to teach these skills, educators can drastically decrease discipline issues, truancy prob-

---

The Kid in Purple Pants

Structured Approaches to Educating Underprivileged Students

lems, and cultural conflicts. Not only does SEL help educators do a better job of educating, but it also allows for students to utilize skills that are not often learned at such a young age. I know I would have greatly benefited from having negotiating skills, empathy, and tolerance. And I'm positive a little SEL education would definitely have kept my brothers out of a lot of fights.

Let me suggest that SEL education is the newest sensation since the dawn of geometry and phonics. Haven't we all known that person, when we were in high school or even college, who was exceptionally smart but didn't have the ability to function in society? That person who was an emotional wreck and, because of it, dropped out of school? It is no secret that teaching students how to be loving, caring individuals is important. It is also true that students who prosper in school do so because they are socially and emotionally stable. It's hard to imagine that it took this long to figure that out. In order to do anything correctly, one must be mentally stable. Students are no different. We must educate our students on how to cope with problems, deal with peer pressure, resolve conflicts, and be civic-minded and want to accomplish things for the better good. If we instill in our children these values and ethics, they will flourish and find a means to be better citizens and productive members of our society.

The benefit of our program is nothing new. In the early 1990s, Central School established a "fight-free" school program that charged students with finding alternative ways of coping with anger and teaching a means of conflict resolution that did not involve physical altercation. The program was a huge success at preventing fights among our students. To this day I still love watching our students, many of whom, after learning a few coping skills, calm themselves down by simply counting to 10 before reacting to an adverse situation. This

The Kid in Purple Pants

Structured Approaches to Educating Underprivileged Students

simply-taught lesson has allowed many students to stay in school rather than fight and be suspended. I do not subscribe to the analogy that a child must first touch the stove in order to know it is hot. We can teach our students how to cope with stress, manage anger, and be cognizant of why they might be feeling and behaving in the manner they are.

As part of our SEL program, we have established a community service project. We encourage our students to be a part of a debris-recycling program, which consists of students, parents, and community volunteers banding together to recycle local landscape debris to be reused in our community garden. The project has let our students be involved in the betterment of our community, while at the same time making them better individuals. Students have developed a sense of pride in working hard to make their community a better place to live. The pride that each student and teacher feels after a hard day's work is awesome to see. These aren't just ordinary students. These are students who have been angry and frustrated with society. Students who feel as though the city, the police, and teachers are always after them. These are students who have altered their mind frames and changed the way they feel about helping others. It is a big accomplishment. Students who would have ordinarily spent a Saturday morning finding a way to steal from the local Wal-Mart are now working in a community project that will help provide tomatoes and fresh vegetables to a local food pantry during the summer.

Knowing What they Need:

> • The most important element in a good social and emotional learning (SEL) program, as in everything

The Kid in Purple Pants

Structured Approaches to Educating Underprivileged Students

with education, is the teacher. Hiring, training, and leading teachers to be caring, understanding, and knowledgeable educators of the benefits of SEL is vital.

- Provide the needed professional development to the entire school staff (e.g., teachers, administrators, custodians, secretaries, cafeteria workers, volunteers). Everyone must be a part of creating an environment of emotional stability.

- Choose a curriculum that works for your school. A program is only as good as it is utilized and supported. A curriculum that cannot be used effectively is of little use when wanting to create systematic change.

- Make your program visible through posters, local newspaper coverage, newsletters, etc.

- Celebrate successes! Announce weeks without a fight, make special announcements about extraordinary acts of kindness from students and staff, etc.

Character Education

Like almost every other educator who has ever been forced to participate in *another* school-wide initiative, when I first heard of character education, Positive Behavior Interventions and Supports (PBIS), and SEL, I thought it was all a bunch of bull. How could we possibly be responsible for teaching all the academics we needed to teach, play sports, prepare kids for college, and at the same time make sure that we never hurt a student's feelings and still have all of our students be in complete touch with their feelings? I was a non-believer. I had come from the school of hard knocks. My students did not

The Kid in Purple Pants

Structured Approaches to Educating Underprivileged Students

necessarily need to like me, but above all else they needed to respect me. And how I got them to respect me, even if it meant screaming, hollering, and threatening, was better than possibly losing them by allowing them to do whatever they wanted.

"I don't REWARD good behavior, I EXPECT it," was one of the first comments I remember making after being told my school was thinking of instituting a positive behavior program. Why in the world would I reward students every time they did the right thing? Would I have to reward them for doing their homework, for getting a drink without pushing in line, for smiling and acting happy? It went against everything I had ever found that defined success in a classroom. I yelled and I got respect. I could easily allow a student to leave my room and never come back. It didn't matter to me that these students might have issues that made them irresponsible, made them act out, or made them be late for my class. None of those things mattered to me. I was teaching some important material and if a student did not want to be part of it, good riddance.

I was making some serious mistakes in my classroom.

In schools where high poverty and high mobility exist, positive behavior and SEL programs are a must. What better way to prepare students for a day of school than to teach them what is expected? So many underprivileged students come to school with no knowledge of how to behave in a structured environment. Many have never attended preschool, gone to summer camp, or ever had to quietly sit through a movie. Being loud, doing what they want and when they want is the norm for many students. This is not how we do business in schools. So for those students, teaching these expectations is a necessity.

The Kid in Purple Pants

Structured Approaches to Educating Underprivileged Students

For those who argue that these tools for success should be taught at home, I agree. There is nothing I would love more than parents parenting and teaching students expectations and responsibility. It would be great. It would mean that teachers would truly only have to teach subjects and that students would come to school ready to learn. It sure would make for more time for academics. But, in fact, these skills for success in school are not being taught.

We would *definitely* teach a student his or her colors if he or she came to school unprepared with this knowledge. If a student in third grade couldn't read, the radar would go off and we would find a means of getting that student back on track. We would intervene and give the extra help.

But a child who comes to us a little rambunctious, who won't sit in his chair, and will not stop cussing and wanting to do what he wants when he wants? We kick him out, put him in an alternative placement, or possibly label him as a student with special needs. My, "I don't reward good behavior, I expect it," standard didn't work for me. I expected good behavior, but if I had not taught them what I wanted, how could I truly know if someone understood? Would I have expected a student who had been absent the day before to know what had been taught? Would I expect them to be able to master this concept without it being taught? Was there a possibility that they may know what I had taught?

Yes! But I couldn't assume this. I would be forced to teach the concept. For many of our students, close to 85% of them, what I was expecting was already known. They understood and would follow the rules because they knew, as Ruby Payne would state, the "unwritten rules" of school. But for the 15% of my students who did not know these rules, my expectation that they know and understand was hindering their ability to learn and my ability to be an effective teacher.

The Kid in Purple Pants

Structured Approaches to Educating Underprivileged Students

What Character Education Looks Like in School:

- Mandate that character education be a part of everyday practices in your school. A hit-or-miss approach to teaching good character will not produce the results that bring about long-term change in how our students understand the importance of moral fiber.
- Be rigorous in creating your character education curriculum. Remember, as educators, we would never take a lackadaisical approach to mathematics or reading.
- Create blocks of time specifically for character education.
- Develop incentives for students that keep good character a focal point in the school. For example, have "Character Student of the Month" assemblies, celebrate character successes in newsletters, and build a good relationship with local newspapers so they will highlight your successes in the media.
- Purchase, borrow, or even create a scientific-based curriculum with proven results.
- Be a good example. As educators and administrators we are always in the spotlight. If we can't control, express, and maintain our emotions in a proper way, how can we hold our students to those expectations?
- Change the perception many students hold about school. Prior to introducing academics, begin the year with listening, team building, and any activity that helps build a culture of unity and trust. A good program will ultimately create a loving, caring family atmosphere throughout the school.

The Kid in Purple Pants

Structured Approaches to Educating Underprivileged Students

I remember one of my first conversations with Marijon Stites. She was the veteran science teacher who no student, or teacher for that matter, would ever cross at Lake Crest Elementary. Marijon had been appointed my unofficial "mentor" for my first year, and we occupied the only two rooms in the hallway closest to the gym. She was a tough woman who had grown up on a dairy farm in central Illinois and had worked hard for everything she had ever gotten. She worked her way through college, paying for everything herself, married right out of school, and began a teaching career. She loved her work and, still to this day, I have never met another teacher who prepared better for a day's worth of lessons than Marijon.

Marijon was dedicated to making certain that students were absorbing what she was teaching. She would teach "bell to bell," and each student would pay close attention to everything she wrote on the blackboard or showed on her overhead projector. As a first-year teacher, I idolized Marijon. She had her act together and I didn't. She had the respect of every student in her class. They never acted up, she never gave out detentions, and she was always busy with schoolwork. I, on the other hand, didn't have the respect of all my students. I was constantly telling them to be quiet, gave out my fair share of detentions, and would go home empty-handed at night because I was too tired to do anything but sit in front of the TV and try to forget why I had not been all that effective at anything that day.

It was early October and I suspected Marijon was at her wit's end with me. (She may have also been prompted by our principal to give me a firm talking-to; I cannot be sure.) She walked into my classroom at the end of another long, detention-filled day complete with a host of screaming matches and idle threats. Marijon, who never minced words, marched up to

The Kid in Purple Pants

Structured Approaches to Educating Underprivileged Students

my desk and said, "Anderson, you aren't going to make it unless you change the way you are doing things." What did that old lady just say to me? I was cool. The kids liked me. I was the golf coach. How could this woman who, seemingly to me, had no relationship with her students, be telling me that I needed to clean up my act? Sure, I had some discipline problems, but I wasn't that bad. Or was I?

Marijon knew I wasn't getting what she was preaching so she continued on, a little more pointed: "You are not their friend. They don't want to be your friend. To them, you are old. Yes, Anderson, even to your seniors, your tired 23-year-old butt is old."

I was having a hard time with this conversation. Granted, I knew I had a few things to iron out when it came to teaching, but I didn't realize that it was so glaring. At 23, I was fast learning that my suit of armor and white horse were nowhere to be found. I was still not able to admit that I needed to change the way I was doing business in my classroom. Marijon continued, "You don't have to be their friend to get their respect. You have to respect them by demanding they give their all to you."

What she was saying was making sense, but I had no clue on how to do it. Every time I was nice to my students, they went nuts. If I gave them 10 minutes of free time, it always ended with me yelling and screaming that it was getting too loud and we all need to sit down and get silent. Or worse, I would promise a "movie day" if everyone behaved for a few days and then, when a few kids didn't behave, the ones who had behaved got angry, complained, and thought I was a no-good liar. This, in actuality, was true for them. They had done nothing wrong, followed the rules, and now were not getting the movies they deserved because of the bad behavior of others. I asked Marijon how I was supposed to "respect" these

The Kid in Purple Pants

Structured Approaches to Educating Underprivileged Students

kids? "Teach them what you want. If giving kids free time is your thing, which I think is stupid, but, hey, it's your thing, then teach them what you expect from them," she explained. Teach them how to sit down and talk quietly? Doesn't take a brain surgeon to know what that looks like. Why in the world would I need to teach them that?

Marijon was smart enough to also praise her young ingé-nue. She told me that I knew my subject matter, was intelligent, had good ideas, and was creative in differentiating my instruction. (She didn't say "differentiate'; I think her exact words were "mixing things up some.") After finishing building me up, she went back to explaining the things I needed to do to make my students successful. She said I needed to explain my expectations, praise *only* when it was appropriate, and, most important, *never* try to bribe students. She said they see bribery as a sign of weakness and would eat me alive if I kept it up.

I have to admit that I never really understood *exactly* what Marijon was trying to tell me. What she told me did wake me up, however, and forced me become a whole lot stricter with my students. Soon I started teaching "bell to bell" and tried to be anything but a friend to many of my students. I didn't want to lose my job, and I had sensed from Marijon that if I didn't change my ways, that might be the road I was heading down.

I quickly learned to intimidate students into doing what I wanted them to do. When I taught, I gave no personal anecdotes, told almost nothing of myself, and would demand silence. I was glad my students had no clue that I was twice as afraid of them as they were of me. During this same time, I would have bad dreams at night that my classroom would become completely unruly and the principal would be forced to come in and settle down my students. I hated that dream and it

The Kid in Purple Pants

Structured Approaches to Educating Underprivileged Students

only escalated the disciplined way I treated my students to make certain they were never out of line.

Now, when I reflect on those days, I realize that Marijon was not telling me to be mean and intimidating to my students. She was simply telling me to make my expectations clear. I needed to let them know what was expected of them when it came to their behavior. Marijon was always quick to praise her students and had a good relationship with parents.

Marijon, although the concept didn't have a special name, had been using positive behavior interventions since the early 1970s. Her approach to educating brought her much success and even more triumphs for her students. She had an extremely successful teaching career that consisted of a state championship in Envirothon (a science academic competition), in which I was considered her assistant coach because we had to stay overnight in Monticello, Illinois, and the boys on the team needed a chaperone. I still tout that "state championship" assistant coach title on my résumé. Marijon had the love and respect of her students, and I often saw students coming back to her room after graduating and telling her how easy their freshman biology class had been first semester. Why the success? Marijon had mastered teaching expectations in an environment that was proactive, not reactive. The second a student walked into Marijon's classroom he knew what his teacher would expect from him that day, what would be allowed and what would not be allowed, and had the peace of mind that she would respect him and appreciate him for doing what was outlined for him in his quest for knowledge. Students want structure. They yearn for it, especially when they are a little afraid, confused, or apprehensive.

A stress-free, positive environment is what an underprivileged student needs. A stressful home life where tempers flare quickly and anxiety is constantly unsettling is something a

The Kid in Purple Pants

Structured Approaches to Educating Underprivileged Students

poor student should not also endure at school. Sadly, this is exactly what many students face as they walk through the school doors.

The program is not a patchwork; rather, it's a school-wide approach that addresses the needs of all students in the school, in classrooms, and every other facet of the school environment (hallways, restrooms, offices, etc.). The entire school works together to teach the expectations, and each is consistent with the message of what is expected. Nothing is left to chance when it comes to providing students with a clear picture of what is expected of them while in school. The model is a 100% proactive approach that reinforces and also recognizes students who are able to model the behaviors necessary for success in school. It also ensures that systems are in place to help those students who need additional support. A tiered system allows for a variety of interventions to be utilized to meet the needs of a variety of students. The approach is systematic and it consistently acknowledges appropriate behavior in an attempt to show recognition for achievements and success.

The model is also data driven. All discipline data is collected and analyzed in an attempt to better understand where changes in the school environment need to be made in order to effect positive changes in behavior. For example, if it is found that many discipline problems are taking place in the hallways, an analysis of the data will allow for teachers and administrators to intervene and make adjustments to what is needed to remedy the problems occurring in the hallway.

The most important thing to remember about implementing any type of positive behavior program is to not BRIBE. Bribing, as Marijon said, is the easiest way to sabotage your program. PBIS is a means of teaching and changing behaviors. The objective is to teach those behaviors that will benefit students the most in their attempts at learning. It is also in-

The Kid in Purple Pants

Structured Approaches to Educating Underprivileged Students

tended to change behaviors that are detrimental to learning while in a school environment. Bribery does neither of these things. Bribing students to do what a teacher wants is like taking aspirin for a toothache. The aspirin will help ease the pain for a short time, but it will not fix the reason for the toothache. A bribe lasts only as long as it is not paid off. Once paid, it's over and the unwanted behavior will resume.

If a school wants to truly change behavior, these behaviors must become second nature. A habit that is practiced over and over creates success. We can't expect our students to know what we want and expect from them if we do not instill in them the means to be successful. When it comes to testing, we will put as much money as possible into remediation material, extra teachers, and tutoring services. However, there is a stigma that hangs over remediating behavior. For too long we have allowed a mindset to dominate our schools that says that these things should and can only be taught at home. It is the reason character education programs are cut first when making budgetary decisions. Those making the decision to cut the programs are, for the most part, those who feel we can do without because they are capable of providing these skills to their children. These choices are what cause us to continue to have difficulty teaching math and reading. We give up on the programs that set a path that allows for learning. It seems ironic that the first things cut are those that are needed most when trying to teach.

The Kid in Purple Pants

Structured Approaches to Educating Underprivileged Students

**w to Make the Right Choice for Character
lucation and Social Emotional Education?**

ν Do I Decide?" Series of Guidelines was developed to help you make informed decisions that will positively impact young children's challenging behavior and social-emotional development. Today, there are many curricula that focus on young children's social emotional development. Our purpose here is not to recommend certain curricula but rather to offer guidance on how to choose the one that will best meet your needs. It is important to note, however, that CSEFEL believes that every early childhood program should have a social emotional curriculum in place in order to provide a structure and focus that will promote this fundamentally important domain of development.

The Center on the Social and Emotional Foundations for Early Learning (CSEFEL) has also provided some outstanding guidelines for best practices in choosing the right curriculum for a school's needs.

Step #1: Choose a Diverse Team to Provide Input
When choosing a curriculum, a broadly representative team of administrators, direct service providers, and family members should be assembled to provide input. This type of decision-making structure makes it more likely that all interested parties will be committed to the ultimate decision.

Step #2: Have the Team Consider Key Questions
Key questions for teams to consider in order to guide and inform the ultimate curriculum adoption decision are listed below. The questions are organized into two broad categories:

The Kid in Purple Pants

Structured Approaches to Educating Underprivileged Students

A. Pivotal questions designed to address the fundamental issue: "Is this curriculum worthy of more careful review?"

B. Relationship with program characteristics and resources questions, which are designed to help match potentially "acceptable" curriculum to individual program assets and needs.

Pivotal Questions:

1. Has this curriculum been shown to produce scientifically verifiable outcomes?

The team should look for multiple examples of studies published in peer-reviewed journals in which children like the ones of concern were included. Teams need to make certain that the curriculum has been validated with children of similar ages, social-emotional needs, linguistic backgrounds, and culture.

2. Has this curriculum been adopted successfully by programs like ours?

The team should contact similar programs to determine their level of satisfaction with the curriculum. The purpose here is not only to see if fellow providers are "satisfied" but also to inquire about results obtained, problems in implementation and initial training on the materials, and supports needed to assist providers in accurate implementation.

3. Does the curriculum actually impact all of the social-emotional outcomes we are concerned about?

The Kid in Purple Pants

Structured Approaches to Educating Underprivileged Students

Social-emotional curricula vary widely in their scope and therefore their potential impact on children's behavior. Some curricula focus primarily on friendship skills, others on emotional regulation, still others on resolving peer conflicts. Teams need to be clear about their goals for the curriculum. In some cases, teams may well decide to use all or parts of more than one curriculum to meet their needs.

Relationship with Program
Characteristics / Resources Questions

1. What does it take to become fluent in the use of the curriculum?

It is vital to recognize that adopting the very best curriculum does not guarantee good results. Providers must implement the curricula as intended, to the degree it is intended to be delivered. Teams should explore what training might be available to become fluent with the curriculum and whether there are assessment tools that can be used to determine fidelity of implementation. Relatedly, teams may want to explore the degree to which the curriculum is "manualized." If a curriculum is highly prescriptive, providing guidance as to what to say and do and when to say and do it, then it is more likely that a broad range of providers can be successful implementers.

2. What are the costs—in dollars and in time—to implement with fidelity?

Not only are there material costs but curricula differ in terms of relative durability (i.e., wear and tear) and the time and re-

The Kid in Purple Pants

Structured Approaches to Educating Underprivileged Students

lated costs to train staff and maintain fidelity of implementation. Teams need to consider the relative costs and benefits of the curriculum.

3. How will this curriculum fit into the program's current philosophy and practices?

Teams need to evaluate the "goodness-of-fit" between the proposed curriculum and program philosophy. In some cases this will not be an issue, whereas in others the issue may be overwhelming. In some cases the team may decide that the outcomes achievable with adoption are so important that it may necessitate a re-examination of their program philosophy. In any case, the bottom-line issue is increasing the likelihood of "buy-in" by program staff.

Step #3: Promote Buy-In and Implementation Fidelity
Once a curriculum has been selected, the team should take the following steps to promote buy-in and fidelity of implementation:

1. Have a formal "launch" of the curriculum in which all staff and families are informed about the decision-making process, why the particular curriculum was chosen, how providers will be trained, and what outcomes are expected.

2. Schedule training and continue training until staff can implement the curriculum with fidelity. Along the way provide acknowledgment for excellent implementation by individual staff.

3. Determine what steps supervisors will take to support fidelity of implementation. Set up communication channels such that staff can make their support needs heard.

4. Set up a system to evaluate child outcomes, making sure to link this assessment with other ongoing efforts.

The Kid in Purple Pants

Structured Approaches to Educating Underprivileged Students

Source: Center on the Social and Emotional Foundations for Early Learning: www.vanderbilt.edu/csefel

Successful Programs:

Positive Behavioral Intervention and Supports (PBIS): Emphasizes the establishment of organizational supports or systems that give school personnel capacity to use effective interventions accurately and successfully at the school, district, and state levels. These supports include (a) team-based leadership, (b) data-based decision-making, (c) continuous monitoring of student behavior, (d) regular universal screening, and (e) effective ongoing professional development. PBIS is a framework or approach for assisting school personnel in adopting and organizing evidence-based behavioral interventions into an integrated continuum that enhances academic and social behavior outcomes for all students.

PBIS is *not* a packaged curriculum, scripted intervention, or manualized strategy.

Contact: www.pbis.org / Laura Riffel at laura.riffel@pbis.org

Character First! Education:
Character First! Education was brought to life through the commitment and vision of public school and police officials to address the real issues of today's youth. The Character First! Education Series is designed specifically for elementary-age children, pre-kindergarten through sixth grade. The colorful and lively curriculum helps capture children's attention with songs, stores, crafts, games, memory work, object

The Kid in Purple Pants

Structured Approaches to Educating Underprivileged Students

98

lessons, coloring pages, collectible Character Cards, and posters.

Contact:
Character First! Education
520 W. Main Street
Oklahoma City, OK 73102
(405) 815-0001 / Fax: (405) 815-0002
www.characterfirst.com/education/
email: info@characterfirst.com

I CAN Character Curriculum:
Thousands of educators, students, and parents across America are excited about Zig Ziglar's I CAN Character Curriculum. Through I CAN, they are learning not only the ABCs of education, but also more importantly, the ABCs of life: Attitude, Behavior, and Character. Available in two complete curriculums: one for kindergarten through fifth grade, and a second for sixth grade and up.

Contact:
Bob Alexander, President
The Alexander Resource Group
176 Lake View Drive North
Macon, GA 31210
(877) USA-ICAN / Fax: (478) 476-9081
www.yesican.net
email: bob@yesican.net

WiseSkills K-2
This character education program is a teacher-friendly and interdisciplinary way to build the character of young people. Innovative and exciting activities are conveniently organized

The Kid in Purple Pants

Structured Approaches to Educating Underprivileged Students

around monthly Character Themes and include: Character Education, Conflict Resolution, Curriculum Integration, Career Awareness, Service-Learning, and Parent/Community Involvement.

Contact:
Seth Schapiro
WiseSkills Resources
P.O. Box 491
Santa Cruz, CA 95061
(888) 947-3754
www.wiseskills.com
email: info@wiseskills.com

Source: The write-ups for each of the character education programs came from their websites.

The Kid in Purple Pants

Structured Approaches to Educating Underprivileged Students

Chapter 6

Time for Academics

"The poverty of our century is unlike that of any other. It is not, as poverty was before, the result of natural scarcity, but of a set of priorities imposed upon the rest of the world by the rich. Consequently, the modern poor are not pitied...but written off as trash. The twentieth-century consumer economy has produced the first culture for which a beggar is a reminder of nothing."

—John Berger

It seems odd to write a book on how to provide poor students a better chance at receiving a quality education, then leaving any talk about academics until the sixth chapter. At the same time, it actually makes a lot of sense. I have found that nothing can be done properly until the person doing it is in the correct frame of mind. Likewise, our students must first be ready to learn and find value in what they are doing.

I have a weight problem. And it's not just an "I gain weight over Christmas break" problem. It's a cruel monkey that resides on my back. I am a stress eater who has fluctuated from 170 pounds to my all-time high of close to 400 pounds. I told you it was a serious problem! My weight has everything to do with how my mind is functioning and what I have going on in my life. When I am stressed, I eat. I maintain my weight and eat healthfully when things are copacetic and I feel I have control of what I am doing.

The Kid in Purple Pants

Structured Approaches to Educating Underprivileged Students

When I left Oakland, Illinois, and moved back home (to southern Illinois), I weighed 230 pounds. One year after starting a new teaching job at Central and eating my way through the stress of not being tenured, I was up to nearly 300 pounds. And it didn't take long to pack it on. After my fourth year at Central and being granted tenure, I again felt secure. I dieted, exercised, and started a new regimen. I weighed 175 pounds one year to the day after being granted tenure. I then became principal and ballooned back up to almost 330 pounds. I have just now started the struggle of losing that weight, but it has not been easy. So, I'm fat, but what's the point? Simply this: If a man is 100% cognizant of what is causing him to have a problem with maintaining his weight and is still helpless at controlling it, how can we expect a student, totally unaware of what might be causing his or her learning or behavioral problems, to be successful in school without giving him or her the proper guidance and support? We are asking children to think like adults, to do something they are not cognitively capable of doing, simply because of their age.

The same is true for any students who have ever tried to concentrate while they are hungry, worried about money, or scared that they don't know where they will be sleeping that night. As in the case of me and my eating habits, poor children need to be in the proper frame of mind before we can effectively educate them on the basic learning standards that all children need to know and understand.

Okay, now that all our students are educated on how to conduct themselves in school; have motivation, self-worth, and pride in their community, and have met their basic, social and emotional needs, it's finally time to start teaching reading and math.

The Kid in Purple Pants

Structured Approaches to Educating Underprivileged Students

Zeroes Aren't Permitted (ZAP)

The Zeroes Aren't Permitted (ZAP) program was initiated because a large population of the student body was not passing classes simply due to their lack of submitting completed homework. With the increasing demands of No Child Left Behind (NCLB) and the consequences of not meeting Adequate Yearly Progress (AYP), the amount of instructional time to teach everything needed just was not feasible. Teachers started to increase the amount of homework to cover more material in order to prepare students for high-stakes, mandated state tests. With this increase in assigned work came an increase in homework coming back to school incomplete. ZAP was implemented to ensure that every student has an opportunity to finish homework and not be permitted to fail by choice.

ZAP is a fairly simple concept. Any student who is not finishing his/her homework must complete that homework during lunch. For example, if a student did not finish his math assignment in time to turn in on Monday morning, the math teacher would staple a ZAP sheet to the assignment and take it down to the ZAP teacher before the student's scheduled lunch. Teachers do not assign a grade for the homework until it is returned to them by the ZAP teacher. If a student does not turn in an assignment, as in the case of a large, extensive project, the teacher is asked to wait five days before finally giving the student a zero. In some cases a student will refuse to finish a project or an assignment and it is necessary to finally assign a zero for the work.

When the student's lunchtime comes about, he would then be greeted at the door of the cafeteria by the ZAP teacher and told to get in line and get his lunch and come to the school's conference room. While in the room, he gets out the assign-

The Kid in Purple Pants

Structured Approaches to Educating Underprivileged Students

ment, logs why he is in ZAP, eats lunch, and works on the missing assignment. An average of two to four students are in each ZAP lunch period. A teacher monitors the work, helps when needed, and maintains a quiet, orderly, and productive work environment. Students who must attend do not receive recess for that day, which is the only punishment associated with the homework not being done. Previously, students who did not do homework would receive a detention after accumulating three unfinished assignments. The number of detentions was astronomical and was not a deterrent for failing to do homework. The same students would receive detention after detention for missing homework. Simply put, even though detentions were being issued and served, the discipline was not changing the fact that the child did not have a support system at home that was monitoring the punishment and making corrections to remediate the lack of homework completion on the child's side. Looking back on this, I feel like an idiot. Did I really think that giving detentions for incomplete homework was going to change the fact that a child came from a single-parent home where it was almost impossible for the parent to monitor and make certain homework was being completed? Would making a student spend an hour after school miraculously change the state of the household and create an environment where the student would now have the support system to be successful? That thought process is embarrassing. To make matters worse, under the old system those same students would have also received a zero for the assignment.

I have long known and observed that many students who come from poor socioeconomic backgrounds do not fare as well in school as students who come from higher income families. I had always assumed that if a student did not do his homework there must have been a good reason. I have learned, after almost 18 years of serving in public education,

The Kid in Purple Pants

Structured Approaches to Educating Underprivileged Students

that homework must have value if it is to be completed. The value of homework may be as simple as increased learning and achievement or less obvious things such as not getting in trouble for incomplete homework or meeting family expectations.

Does ZAP work? Definitely. But it wasn't until a long-time colleague came into my office with tears in his eyes that I realized just how well. Steve looked at me and said he had something important to tell me. I was worried something had happened to a member of his family or he had bad news regarding his health. With his voice cracking slightly, Steve started with, "It's Daniel." Daniel is "one of those students you never forget." Daniel, since kindergarten, had been at least a head taller than all his classmates, a little...no, a lot, clumsier, extremely unorganized, and looked as though he had already celebrated his 20th birthday, although he was only 14. Daniel lived with his grandmother, who worked more jobs and more hours than any human being should ever have to work. The choice wasn't hers; she had children and grandchildren to take care of. Checking Daniel's bag for homework, however, was not going to fit into her already overextended schedule.

It was report card day after the first quarter of implementing ZAP. Daniel had been a repeat visitor to ZAP, and his visits had not always been ideal. On many occasions Daniel would huff and puff his way to the ZAP room and complete his homework, angry and frustrated that he was going to miss an exciting game of touch football or tag. Missing his recess was not something Daniel enjoyed. Several times I spotted him trying to finish his assignment before school as he waited for the morning late bell to ring. This was something I *never* saw Daniel do before ZAP. Daniel enjoyed his free time and didn't really see any use in doing homework because his only

The Kid in Purple Pants

Structured Approaches to Educating Underprivileged Students

dream was to join the military when he got out of school. He saw school as just one more hoop to jump through before getting to join the service and do what he wanted. When Steve gave Daniel his report card, he was extremely surprised by what was said next. Daniel looked up, stared at his teacher, and said, "Mr. Lanter, this is the first time in my life I haven't gotten an F on my report card." Daniel kept looking down at his report card and then back up to Steve almost as if he couldn't believe what he was seeing. Daniel whispered, "Maybe I'm not stupid."

For the first time in Daniel's life he was not allowed to fail himself. He was not given the opportunity to not put forth an effort when it came to his education. He was made to learn. We didn't allow him to make a decision on whether he would learn or not. It seems silly to think that this was the first time in Daniel's life he was not allowed to fail. This was the first quarter of Daniel's life where he didn't hear, "Well, fine, I can't make you do your homework. If you want to fail, I guess that's up to you."

Would society allow children to determine if they were going to take driver's education before getting their license? Could you imagine hearing a teacher say, "Well, fine, I can't make you learn how to drive a car. If you want to go out and drive a car without knowing how, I guess that's up to you." Would we allow a 14-year-old to meet a stranger they met on the Internet because that is what they want to do? "Well fine, I can't make you realize that is not the safest thing to do. If you want to go off with a stranger from the Internet, I guess that's up to you." We would never allow children to determine their own fate on when they are ready to drive a car or how to deal with online predators, but we will allow for a child to determine his own fate when it comes to his education.

The Kid in Purple Pants

Structured Approaches to Educating Underprivileged Students

Schools all across the nation allow for this to be a reality for our children. Our system has been one that has focused more on responsibility than on academic achievement. Our system has determined that the most responsible students are the best. The students with the best home life and most responsible parents are superlative.

A student named Ryan was one of my first realizations that grades might not be all that important. He was a good kid but he would not do his homework. I could not figure him out. He seemed like a smart enough kid, but he wouldn't put any effort into his schooling. I ended up flunking Ryan every quarter I had him. As his literature teacher for both seventh and eighth grade, I assigned Ryan eight F's in literature on his report cards. I told myself over and over that it wasn't my fault. This kid wouldn't do his homework, and the few times I talked with his parents, they didn't seem all that concerned that he was flunking my class.

On Ryan's last day of eighth grade, I handed out the high school placement test results to all my students. I couldn't believe my eyes. I knew something was wrong. There was no way Ryan was the smartest kid in the class. Ryan, by far, exceeded every other student's score. But, what made this whole situation 100 times worse was that I was the only surprised person in the entire classroom. "Mr. Anderson, Ryan is, by far, the smartest kid in the class. Even John knows that," stated Emily with zero apology in her voice. John, whose parents came to every school event, attended every parent/teacher conference, called just to "check in" every quarter, and the student who got the best grades in the class, simply nodded at Emily's comment and went about sharing his test results with his fellow students.

Why in the world hadn't I been able to make Ryan find the value in my class? Why didn't he want to do any of my

The Kid in Purple Pants

Structured Approaches to Educating Underprivileged Students

homework? What was I doing that failed to engage him? If I had forced Ryan to be responsible and show his abilities to me, would I have been more aware of Ryan's needs? Most certainly, I believe. I would have very quickly become aware of Ryan's genius and nurtured those abilities. Hadn't I done that with my other students who had shown talent? I will never forget those endless after-school meetings I would have with my best writers in which we would hone their writing abilities and foster in them a love for going above and beyond simply because they were good at something. I so wish I had given Ryan that same opportunity. How many other students had I missed? I do not want to imagine. Fortunately, today kids like Ryan are not falling between the cracks. We spot them and problem solve why they aren't successful. We dig deep and never give up on them. If I had worked hard to find out why Ryan didn't do his homework, could I have found that he saw no value in doing something he had already mastered and then given him alternative assignments that may have been challenging and thought-provoking for him?

Those who are opposed to ZAP complain that it fosters irresponsibility. Critics state that it allows for students to be negligent and not suffer any consequences for not doing what is expected. They say it is not fair to those students who do their homework on time and put forth the extra effort to finish homework at home.

I truly respect all of these opinions and to some extent agree to them all. There will always be those who take advantage of not having to do their homework on time and use it as a crutch to "get one over" on teachers. It's one of the drawbacks to a program designed to help those students who might not have the time or support to finish homework.

I wholeheartedly agree that schools need to teach responsibility. Without it, students are destined to fall behind, be-

The Kid in Purple Pants

Structured Approaches to Educating Underprivileged Students

come apathetic, and truly not care about school. This is exactly why we started our program. Students are now responsible for homework whether they do it at home or we mandate they do it at school. Students don't have the opportunity to be irresponsible. We give our students a structured, quiet environment, someone to assist if they are having difficulty, and the inability to make an excuse for not doing what they are supposed to do. If anything, ZAP forces students to realize that they must be accountable for their actions.

But it must be pointed out that one glaring reality still rings true even after the launch of our ZAP program. Although it was a surprise to many of our critics, those students who *always* turned in homework on time continued to *always* turn in homework on time. For these students, not turning in homework on time would be worse than smacking a nun. The students who are a little irresponsible and occasionally forgot a homework assignment, well, they still occasionally didn't do their homework. Again, it is the nature of the beast. This describes my son. He is the quintessential fifth-grade boy. He is far more worried about basketball and swim practice, video games, and making fart noises. The occasional missed assignment or misplaced worksheet was something that did not surprise me one single iota. And, not surprisingly, those students who often or never completed homework assignments continued in that manner. These students didn't have a support system at home that made certain a child's book bag was opened and explored. For these students, class projects were not a family affair. No great increase in the number of students taking advantage of the additional time to finish homework occurred. Our data has held true for three years.

However, one important thing has changed. For many students who rarely turn in homework, an understanding that homework can be beneficial and helpful has started to sink in.

The Kid in Purple Pants

Structured Approaches to Educating Underprivileged Students

Our data, and that of many other ZAP schools, shows that once students are given the opportunity to be successful, homework has value and, even without support systems in place at home, students are making an effort to finish homework and grades are improving.

ZAP has served as an eye-opener for many students, like Daniel, who thought they were just not intelligent or smart. They wholeheartedly felt that because they did not do homework, didn't study for tests, and didn't have a support system at home that encouraged them to do their best, that they were not smart. With ZAP, students are realizing they are intelligent. They are capable of doing well and, for the first time in their lives, are experiencing a little taste of academic success. It's hard for children to realize they have potential and ability if they have never been forced to perform. Schools have been allowing these students to never feel the joy of accomplishing a difficult task.

The first time I experienced such joy was when I was 17 years old. I was working on a very difficult roof project almost 30 miles away from my home. I had strict instructions to not leave the job that night until it was finished because we needed to cash out the roof and get the money to the bank. If I didn't get the money, a "butt load" of checks was going to bounce and then we were going to have some serious problems. Of course, things didn't go as planned. We ran into a lot of bad lumber on the roof that needed to be replaced, one of our roofers got sick and went home early, and the dump truck wouldn't start. I was screwed and in danger of not earning the money we so desperately needed. The checks were going to bounce and my Dad was going to be disappointed. I was so scared, but I could see no other option but to make it work. Having no money, I used the plywood that lined the bottom of the dump truck to do the repairs on the bad lumber on the

The Kid in Purple Pants

Structured Approaches to Educating Underprivileged Students

roof. We worked in the dark to finish, making up for being one man down. And finally, one of the guys on the crew figured out how to start the truck by pressing a screwdriver against the alternator to get a spark. And off we were, money in hand. We had done it! That is one of the proudest moments of my life. I had been forced to persevere and do what was needed to make it work. I would have never experienced this joy if it had not been for the fact that I was not given a free pass out of jail. No one had told it was okay to fail that day. No one said, "Fine, if you don't want to get it finished, fine with me, just give up."

Although my story is one of necessity, it still rings true as an analogy for students and finishing homework. The joy one feels after completing a difficult and seemingly unattainable goal creates intrinsic motivation. Pride, self-esteem, and recognition create inherent growth. We must not allow our students to miss out on these experiences.

We have given a free pass to students who have not been driven enough to put forth an effort. National statistics mirror the same results. Students are finding the benefits of homework completion once it is no longer an option but simply another non-negotiable part of school. When not given the option to fail, students don't! Hmm...what a novel idea.

Summer School

I loved teaching summer school. I had class sizes of 8 to 10 kids, and I only taught math and reading. There was no pressure to make sure I taught the "test," and I would create a curriculum that worked for my students' needs, not the needs of the "test." Each day enabled me to capitalize on "teachable moments" because I could do what I wanted and not have to worry about what learning standard I was going to teach be-

The Kid in Purple Pants

Structured Approaches to Educating Underprivileged Students

fore the beginning of March and state testing. If my students didn't understand a math concept or misinterpreted something we had read, I could simply stop my lesson, reteach it, differentiate my instruction, and then reassess. That was something I had little time for when I was trying to cram nine months of curriculum into six months.

Little wonder that my students loved summer school too. We had fun. We took our time and learned at our own pace. It wasn't as if we were trying to make 6 or 8 months worth of gains in 20 days of summer school. We set goals to gain a couple of months in reading comprehension and to "start getting" some of the more complex math concepts the students didn't comprehend during the school year. It was a collaborative effort and because we had assessments and a means of progress monitoring, I saw my students gain in leaps and bounds.

There is no denying that added time in a classroom setting positively influences a child's education. Although we cannot depend on summer school to be the definitive means to end the widening of the achievement gap for poor children, it can be revealed that it has been extremely helpful in boosting student learning in reading and mathematics. Summer school offers a longer school calendar and an opportunity for our students to experience small class sizes, individual instruction, and a very relaxed learning environment. This luxury is something that not many students, rich or poor, ever get to experience.

It is no surprise that many poor students fall even further behind their wealthier counterparts during summer break. Kids who are in the middle-class tax bracket spend their summer break enjoying culturally enriching activities, such as going to museums, taking vacations, and attending summer camps, and have extra time with their parents. On the flipside,

The Kid in Purple Pants

Structured Approaches to Educating Underprivileged Students

for many poor adolescents, summer is spent babysitting for siblings or simply not leaving the neighborhood for weeks on end. Poor kids don't experience much during summer break and giving them the opportunity to come to school, eat a good breakfast, and be in a very comfortable, structured, environment is exactly what many poor students need to maintain what they have learned during the school year. Summer school prevents the achievement gap for poor kids from expanding over the summer "slide."

Don't allow for poor kids to opt out of summer school. Too often poor students are permitted to not attend summer school, even when their needs are the greatest. We often confuse need with want and this can no longer be tolerated.

It is common that summer school is filled with those students whose parents have the loudest voices at PTA meetings or have advocates who have fought for their child to have a place in summer school. I understand these parents and commend them for what they are doing (i.e., caring for their children). As educators and administrators, we all have met and know the parents who are champions for their children and will do anything to ensure that they are successful and get the most out of their educational experiences. We don't have to look for those parents. They will make themselves noticed and will make certain we understand, meet, and go above and beyond when dealing with their children. We are seeking the parent whose phone number changes monthly, who does not attend PTA meetings, and who never volunteers to work in the "fun fair" booth each spring. We must find the parents who hide from us because they want as little exposure of their shortcomings as possible. I have beat on doors and tricked parents into answering the phone by leaving messages that their son or daughter had been hurt. (I didn't technically lie; the student had come to the nurse's office for a bandage.) I am

The Kid in Purple Pants

Structured Approaches to Educating Underprivileged Students

not proud of what we have resorted to in our means of making certain that our most needy students attend summer school. But it works! We no longer allow students who we know need extra help to choose not to attend our summer program. We mandate that any student who is more than six months behind in reading or mathematics attend summer school. Our data, not surprisingly, has shown that many of the students falling in this category also happen to be economically disadvantaged.

Schools do not work hard enough to make certain that those students who need summer school the most are the ones who attend. We no longer see summer school as a perk. It is essential to us if we are to close the achievement gap.

Often as I was putting kids on the bus after summer school, I spotted poor students—who would have benefited greatly from the extra academic time, lunch, and structure—waving to me from their front porches just yards from the front door of the school. They were not attending because they were not encouraged to attend. Simply because of socio-economic background, these students have been allowed to fall between the cracks and fall further and further behind each and every summer. Many of these students were staying home and providing for their families a service no longer available during the school year—childcare. Many of our middle-school students, during summer break, turn into baby-sitters for younger siblings, which makes it very difficult to "mandate" that those middle schoolers attend summer school. One working poor parent informed me that her 12-year-old was saving her close to $200 a week by staying home with her two younger siblings during the summer. The savings were what was going to give them the money to purchase a new car in the fall. How was I going to convince this mother that her child needed to be in summer school when she was instead

The Kid in Purple Pants

Structured Approaches to Educating Underprivileged Students

providing the family with a means of obtaining reliable transportation? I, better than anyone, could understand this. This is a reality we cannot ignore. Although the financial means of doing so is not possible for many schools and districts, we must find a way to remedy this problem. I do believe this is a larger scale problem that needs to be brought to the attention of lawmakers and those who do state funding.

At the end of my first year as a principal, I was ready to have the best summer school ever. I had mandated that any student who performed at more than six months behind grade level in either reading or math attend summer school. Also, all students who were classified as free or reduced lunch eligible were "recommended" for summer school. By that, I meant they were not "required" to attend but that the extra help would be a benefit and could keep the child from falling behind. It was my way of trying to make our disadvantaged parents understand that we were here to help and that summer school was not a bad thing.

I was surprised to find that many parents considered summer school was for bad kids who were being punished for not doing what they were supposed to do during the regular school year. After sending out summer school letters, I received phone calls from parents inquiring as to why a child "who had never been in trouble" was mandated to attend summer school. It takes a lot of talking, patience, and educating to explain to parents that summer school is for remediation, maintaining what was learned during the year, and enrichment, and is not a "bad" thing that is a punishment. Parents must understand that additional time in school is not for children who do not know how to behave; rather it is for students who need the additional support, smaller class sizes, and individual attention.

The Kid in Purple Pants

Structured Approaches to Educating Underprivileged Students

To make certain that parents are educated and understand the benefits of summer school, we are scheduling parent/teacher conferences in the spring, in addition to the fall. This additional conference during late March can do wonders in laying the groundwork for educating parents about summer school. At fall conferences inform parents that the benefits of summer school will be discussed during the spring conference and a decision on whether a child would attend would be determined then as well.

Technology

"Mr. Anderson, thank you, I want to show my mom the Internet. She has never seen it before, and she is thirty years old," were the words that made me realize that all the long hours, hard work, and money we invested in our 1:1 computer program (every child in our middle school has his or her own computer) were well worth it. These words came from a seventh-grader who lived in a trailer park with his single mother and two brothers. He was talking about the first day he was able to take his MacBook home from school. He was very smart and his love of knowledge and drive to do well were reason enough to know why he loved the Web. This computer was his opportunity to share the world with her. His excitement and thirst to share this extraordinary tool were inspiring. Josh knew he had been given something that his mother could never provide for him or his siblings.

In a world where technological advances never cease to amaze, many of our families were being left behind. Technology is expensive and difficult to obtain and maintain for underprivileged families. Providing all of our middle school students with their own computers has enabled them to explore technology in a whole new way. We have provided our stu-

The Kid in Purple Pants

Structured Approaches to Educating Underprivileged Students

dents an opportunity to be teachers to their parents. Coincidentally, our wireless network connection reaches to the adjacent trailer park and allows those students to maintain Internet connect at home. Bonus!

Technology for Teachers:

> - Utilize technology to change the roles of teachers and students. Make the student the center of attention. Project-based assessments and cooperative learning approaches help students to be innovative and define goals for their own learning.
> - Allow students to work collaboratively while making use of technology. Students who work together to accomplish a common goal experience the rewards of teamwork.
> - Students do not see technology as something to be afraid of. Technology is what they know and understand. Technology is fun.
> - Technology opens a window to the world. The more information we make available to our students, the more they will explore it.
> - 75% of all jobs in America require the use of a computer in one capacity or another. Get your students ready for the job market.
> - Seek grants that allow for advancements in technology. Money for public schools is scarce, so you must go in search for it if you hope to find it.

Giving a student a computer and expecting it to be the answer to all the world's problems, is, unfortunately, not reality. Allowing for students to simply explore the computer, play

The Kid in Purple Pants

Structured Approaches to Educating Underprivileged Students

games, and take notes is not enough. Teachers must be trained on how to use the technology to its fullest advantage. Expecting a textbook-based curriculum, enriched by technology, to be the answer to our problems, is not enough. A total realignment of curriculum is needed. The resources, instructional strategies, assessment methods, and scope and sequence utilized all need to be tweaked. We cannot expect our students to grow into critical thinkers if we do not allow for the technology to advance new and innovative teaching strategies. Do we still use a strict standards-aligned curriculum? Most certainly. However, because we have learned to allow students to assess themselves through the use of project-based assessments, our students have now learned what it means to earn a grade.

Great Technology Resources for the Classroom:

http://glogster.com/explore
A Glog is an interactive visual platform in which users create a "poster" or "web page" of multimedia elements, including text, audio, video, images, graphics, drawings, and data.

http://mste.illinois.edu/about
The Mathematics, Science, and Technology Education (MSTE) program at the University of Illinois at Urbana-Champaign is a community that promotes collaboration between widely dispersed academic researchers, K–12 school teachers, administrators, and students at all levels, as well as supportive interactions with a board of experienced advisors.

The Kid in Purple Pants

Structured Approaches to Educating Underprivileged Students

http://nlvm.usu.edu/en/nav/vlibrary.html
The National Library of Virtual Manipulatives (NLVM) is an NSF-supported project to develop a library of interactive, web-based virtual manipulatives or concept tutorials—mostly in the form of Java applets—for mathematics instruction (emphasis on K–2). The project includes dissemination and extensive internal and external evaluation.

http://www.edutopia.org/
The George Lucas Educational Foundation is dedicated to improving the K–12 learning process by documenting, disseminating, and advocating for innovative, replicable, and evidence-based strategies that prepare students to thrive in their future education, careers, and adult lives.

http://www.khanacademy.org/
The Khan Academy is a not-for-profit organization with the goal of changing education for the better by providing a free world-class education to anyone anywhere. All of the site's resources are available to anyone—student, teacher, home-schooler, or principal.

http://www.sitesforteachers.com
This website contains links to other sites that contain resource and educational material, and the sites are ranked by popularity.

The Kid in Purple Pants

Structured Approaches to Educating Underprivileged Students

Tutoring

One only need do a minimal amount of research to find that students who come from poor homes are not as prepared for school as their well-to-do counterparts. We have Head Start, and Early Head Start helps prepare our poor students for school. We try our hardest to counter the effects of poverty and how it gives our students a difficult road to follow as they enter school with other students who are far more ready to start a structured academic environment. One of the most effective and easiest ways of countering the effects of poverty is after-school tutoring. An additional ninety minutes of instruction and resource for many students is all they need to succeed.

By providing additional time for needy children, schools can give them the additional resources that are needed to be successful. We can no longer pretend that providing poor students with the same amount of academic instruction will enable them to catch up with students who come from affluent homes. Adequate time is important, and the ability to give disadvantaged students instruction in small class sizes that are focused on remediating specific deficiencies is important and extremely beneficial.

If students aren't having their book bags opened, agendas read, and homework getting finished and explained, then it must be done at school. I do not need to quote research that proves poor parents aren't always able or willing to make education a priority. It's not that they do not equally care about their children. Because of their economic situation, these parents may not have the means or will to do so.

A well-organized after-school program can allow for the development of study habits and organizational skills that poor students can utilize for the rest of their lives. Once again,

The Kid in Purple Pants

Structured Approaches to Educating Underprivileged Students

small class sizes in an environment that is open and free of judgmental peers can do wonders for a student's self-confidence.

The time can also be divided to meet the child's needs in a variety of ways. Utilizing 30 minutes for doing homework and organizing assignments and then using the rest of the time to remediate with direct instruction of standards is a good practice.

Time dedicated for tutoring cannot turn into glorified babysitting. This time must remain structured and be just as formal as the regular school day. A rigorous approach to completing homework and remediating deficiencies must remain a top priority. Like our general curriculum, our after-school tutoring program has a structured curriculum that focuses on the Illinois Learning Standards, and students are progress monitored to make certain the practices we use are making change in our students.

There is also something to be said for "not having any homework." I absolutely love hearing the words "I don't have any homework" stream from my son's mouth. No stress. No worry about him not understanding and me having to review, explain, and make sure he finishes it and has it ready for the next day. In homes where long hours at work make family time a valued commodity, the absence of the extra stress is appreciated. It seems so elementary but it is a real benefit. If two professional educators and an honor student big sister get frustrated trying to help a fifth-grade boy with his spelling words, how must a single mother working midnights feel trying to do the same thing? Taking just one thing off the plate of an already stressed parent can pay big dividends to a family.

The Kid in Purple Pants

Structured Approaches to Educating Underprivileged Students

The greatest of evils and the worst of crimes is poverty.

George Bernard Shaw

The Kid in Purple Pants

Structured Approaches to Educating Underprivileged Students

Chapter 7

Changing the Way We Think About Education

"Public education is the key civil rights issue of the 21st century. Our nation's knowledge-based economy demands that we provide young people from all backgrounds and circumstances with the education and skills necessary to become knowledge workers. If we don't, we run the risk of creating an even larger gap between the middle class and the poor. This gap threatens our democracy, our society and the economic future of America."

—Eli Broad

It doesn't take a PhD in education to notice that many aspects of public education must change if we are to better instruct our children. It isn't that we do not attempt to meet the needs of students. I think that as a society we understand the importance of providing all students a quality education. When I look at polls of what Americans feel are the important issues facing our society, education consistently makes it toward the top of the list. However, the challenge is getting non-educators to understand that problems in education are sometimes more of a societal mind frame that prevents large-scale changes from occurring. There are some huge problems with school funding, equity, high-stakes testing, and the demands of an ever-changing need for educated citizens for the workforce.

The Kid in Purple Pants

Structured Approaches to Educating Underprivileged Students

School Financing

Let me excerpt from a chapter in another book, "Life on the Mississippi: East St. Louis, Illinois," which is the first chapter of *Savage Inequalities* by Jonathan Kozol. In that one chapter Kozol better illustrates the need for change in how we meet the needs of our most underprivileged students than any other author who has tackled the topic. It is almost impossible to fathom life in East St. Louis, Illinois, without ever experiencing it firsthand. It is—as Kozol describes it—heartbreaking. I admit that I do not have personal knowledge of life in East St. Louis, but many of my students do. What I *have* experienced is the East St. Louis educational system and the subsequent effects it has on students and parents. The school district where I work is less than 10 miles from East St. Louis. The few lucky students whose parents were able to move out of East St. Louis to nearby O'Fallon have become some of my district's greatest poverty success stories. These are East St. Louis honor students who come with report cards full of A's and yet are unable to refrain from using foul language or fighting because someone "disrespected" them.

The difficulties facing the district are astronomical. I won't pretend to know which steps must be taken to remedy these problems. But we can no longer allow for a district with nearly 100% of its students living in poverty to be treated the same way as a district facing virtually no poverty. It doesn't make sense. Is it plausible that the same systems for funding and accountability are supposed to fit two school districts that are polar opposites? We can't expect things to change in our poor communities until we acknowledge the disparities and change the system. If I am ever lucky enough to have someone read this book and take offense to its message, I hope that

The Kid in Purple Pants

Structured Approaches to Educating Underprivileged Students

he or she will grind their teeth, stomp around, and get irate, while perhaps spewing, "That Anderson is nuts! We spend more money educating poor kids than any other group of kids in this country. We give those poor kids free lunches. I'm sick of my tax money going to help those kids." I want people to get fired up, but I also want to point out that their immediate reaction is flawed. East St. Louis was once a thriving town in Illinois with some of the largest and most productive cattle houses and railroad junctions in the country. Today that once-vibrant city is better known as the armpit of America. I am not defending the many and immeasurable problems that exist within the city. The corruption, lies, and irresponsible leadership are inexcusable. You know a city has problems when it negotiates with criminals to not steal the copper tubing from air conditioning units. But what might be surprising to many people is that taxpayers in East St. Louis pay higher school property taxes than any other school district in all of St. Clair County. The average levy for a district in St. Clair County is $3.10. In East St. Louis, taxpayers pay almost double that—close to $6. It is very difficult for me to accept that the poor do not pay their fair share when it comes to educating our youth. When schools are funded through local property taxes, it deems that children get the quality of education that the city can afford, not what should be given. In essence, this form of funding means that if you live in an affluent community, you have access to one type of education, but if you live in an impoverished community, you get an inferior version. That statement underlines exactly why the system is broken. The East St. Louis School District is not the only district facing enormous problems. Schools in St. Louis, Kansas City, Detroit, and a host of other financially strapped districts across the nation are encountering these same issues. Any district that is forced to educate students based on the affluences of

The Kid in Purple Pants

Structured Approaches to Educating Underprivileged Students

local tax revenue is at a distinct disadvantage when trying to educate its children.

Although funding mechanisms are not changing, things are turning around in East St. Louis. Through a state takeover, new leadership and accountability practices are being instituted. I look forward to the day that the best things coming out of East St. Louis aren't the football and track teams. What I am most hopeful for is a day when all children have an equal opportunity to receive a quality education that is based on a fair system that levels the playing field for everyone.

Social Equity

As I look back on what I experienced as a young adult, I realize quickly that everything my parents tried to expose us to was their unique approach to providing their children with a little social equity. Although the term is somewhat ambiguous and connotes something different to each person, for my sake, and the sake of those we are trying to educate, it can be defined simply as providing each student with the same opportunities that foster growth, such as going to art museums and having access to public facilities. This is a fairly simple concept, yet it has been nearly impossible to achieve.

I was 14 years old the first time I saw the Gulf of Mexico. I remember like it was yesterday. My entire family was packed into a rented passenger van. Because there were seven of us, my youngest brother sat on someone's lap the entire 14-hour drive.

For the first time in my life, I could see myself somewhere on a map that wasn't within a couple miles of my hometown of Wood River, Illinois. I was walking on the edge of the United States! I had many firsts on that trip: the taste of salt water, the feel of sand squishing between my toes, the

The Kid in Purple Pants

Structured Approaches to Educating Underprivileged Students

smell of seaweed, and the sound of waves crashing into the shore. I saw a real ship and palm trees and exotic wildlife. I learned what life was like for my counterparts as I saw children my own age digging for clams and catching fish they were taking home to their families. It was like a version of how I would cross the levy to the Mississippi River and wade in the overflow ponds and pull out yellow-bellied catfish and giant carp to take home for my own family. I was experiencing culture and a different way of life during my four days in Biloxi, Mississippi. Were my parents giving their children an experience that was both enjoyable and educational? You bet. That trip gave me intrinsic motivation, for once I returned home I went straight away to the local library to study the vast coastal way of life that exists across America. Would I have had this need to learn about life on the bayou if my parents had not allowed us to explore the beaches of Biloxi? I don't believe so.

Social Capital

Social capital is difficult to define. In the business world, capital (money) is what one needs to manufacture and market products. Capital is what gives an entrepreneur the ability to achieve his goal and be successful in business. Social capital is simply a process within society that promotes development for all within the populace.

For the sake of education, however, I like to define social capital as something obtained and reserved by students when exposed to a variety of cultures, social norms, economic existences, and any experience that may enhance their understanding of society's opportunities. Much like an entrepreneur, students use social capital to give them societal knowledge that will help them function in the real world. For poor students,

The Kid in Purple Pants

Structured Approaches to Educating Underprivileged Students

this knowledge may not be afforded them because of their socio-economic status.

Examples of Providing Social Capital:

> • Schedule field trips. Provide opportunities for students to go to museums, civic events, local colleges, theaters, etc. This is the best way of providing social capital.
> • Never take anything for granted as a valuable, teachable topic. Teach students about banking, investing, how the stock market works, art, music, poetry, local government functions, etc.
> • Be proactive. If you can't take students to the capital, bring the capital to them by inviting local government officials into your school, hosting a blood drive, forming an after school fitness program, providing meeting space for local organizations (have students volunteer at those events), or establishing a voter-registration committee (involve students in the process).
> • Create a community/school volunteer program. Involve students in a community garden, recycling program, service project, etc.
> • Get students involved in community activities such as local theater, sports, community organizations, politics, etc.

The social capital I earned on that trip has lasted a lifetime. Social capital and its influence on a child's ability to critically think are sometimes overlooked in the world of education. We cannot dismiss the fact that the more a child ex-

The Kid in Purple Pants

Structured Approaches to Educating Underprivileged Students

periences the wider his scope of the world. I am always amazed at how advanced many of our military children are when it comes to the cultures and beliefs of the different states and countries they have experienced while moving around the world with their military families. These experiences are vast and help them understand the world a little better than many other students who have experienced only a little more than what they can see from their own backyards. Again, it's imperative to give all of our students an equal opportunity at success when it comes to social capital.

The summer school program in my district is composed of not only remediation in academic areas, but we also provide our poorest students with a summer enrichment program. Because we take the extra time and effort to properly report the amount of homeless students in our district, we have been the recipients of additional funds for our disadvantaged students. These resources have helped with transportation costs, teacher salaries, and additional field trips to art museums and the zoo. We have given these experiences to our students that would have never been afforded to them if it had not been for the additional work and effort of our staff. Just recently, our district was awarded an additional $2,000 to help with transportation costs for our summer program. Why? We received this funding simply because we presented our program to members of the state board and our local regional office of education. We were proactive in showcasing to them what we were doing for our less fortunate students. Because we were proactive, when some additional funds became available, we were the first school they thought of because they considered our efforts to be making a difference in the lives of our students.

Social equity comes in different kinds of currency. It can pay dividends by providing professional development to those who need it most. As I already reported, the average student is

The Kid in Purple Pants

Structured Approaches to Educating Underprivileged Students

not the average teacher. This is not the teachers' fault, and blame for not understanding the intricate world of poverty should not be cast upon them. Understanding all the different aspects and nuances of poverty takes time, energy, and money. One cannot expect to understand the norms and beliefs of people not of the same social class. We have invested in providing this knowledge to our teachers. The training and workshops have made our teachers aware of the vast difference between them and some of their students. What's more, a complete understanding of the priorities of different classes has been achieved by most of our staff. Before training, some teachers may have mistaken the fact that a student didn't complete a homework assignment or return a signed permission slip as laziness or stubbornness. Now, these same teachers will first seek out the reasons before resorting to punishment and find new ways of ensuring that all students have a fair shot at a quality education. Our staff no longer adheres to the belief that poverty is always brought on by apathy, low intelligence, and lack of effort; they understand that discrimination, educational disadvantages, and low wages are also causes for poverty. This understanding has produced a staff that looks for ways to fight the effects of poverty on education and create an atmosphere that, despite its disadvantages, promotes learning for all students regardless of their background. Any school wanting to effect similar change should remember the following points:

* Assemble faculty and administration committed to helping all students produce competent work.

* Social equity comprises providing tutoring, mentoring, differentiated instruction, and social and emotional stability to all students.

The Kid in Purple Pants

Structured Approaches to Educating Underprivileged Students

* Teachers understand and appreciate that all students have different learning styles (i.e., differentiate instruction to give all students an equal opportunity to do their best).

* Constantly look to improve programs, curriculum, and assessments that improve student learning.

* Co-taught classrooms give students with disabilities equal access to learning environments that are least restrictive.

* Schools with equity work to lower suspension rates and are proactive in finding interventions that keep students in school, engaged, and respectful of the school environment.

* An appreciation of diversity is a top priority.

* Everyone's opinions, ideas, and culture are appreciated and celebrated.

* Data related to referrals and suspensions are regularly analyzed in an effort to better find where the school is not meeting the needs of its students. Data analysis helps find unproductive rules, problems with routines, and even can help find those teachers who may be using punishments to excess. (An indulgence in having to punish students is a sign of not knowing how to create a positive learning environment.)

* Staff members do not use negative labels, speak condescendingly, or talk about students in negative ways.

* Teachers are advocates for students and should thrive on helping all students to be successful no matter how difficult.

The Kid in Purple Pants

Structured Approaches to Educating Underprivileged Students

The job of a teacher should never be lost because of frustration, anger, or ignorance.

A Changing Workforce

Can the United States continue to educate its youth in the same fashion it has for the last 75 years? It has been a fairly good system and the results have earned dividends that created the greatest society in the world. It has fashioned the strongest economies, many of the greatest minds, and, in my opinion, the most creative and unique individuals in the world. But can this Industrial-age system maintain itself in an evolving environment where students are no longer looking to "just get a job"? Long gone are the days of standing outside a labor hall and being recruited to work in a refinery or factory for 35+ years. We can no longer allow our poor students to fail and become those individuals who do the work that no one else wants to do. It's not right to predetermine a child's fate based on his social background and economic status.

My Dad often (and I mean *often*) tells the story of his cousin Eva. Eva Bell was a very smart, very poor little girl. Her dad was in prison, so she was living with my father's family while things in her immediate family got straightened out (which they never did). Evidently, during the big "How many words can you make out of the word 'Christmas'" contest, the teacher had predetermined that Tom, the son of a doctor, was going to win the challenge even though Eva had made the most words. The only problem was the entire class, led by my father, saw the injustice being served and started chanting, "Eva, Eva, Eva," until the teacher relented and awarded her the prize. That teacher had predetermined Eva's fate. She was poor, her prison-cell dad was most definitely not

The Kid in Purple Pants

Structured Approaches to Educating Underprivileged Students

a doctor, and her mom wasn't the room mother who had brought the prize for the winner of the contest.

For the last 20 years or so, the job market has not tolerated our system of education. It's no secret that the educational systems across the world are outperforming ours and are doing a better job of preparing their children for a post-industrial economy. Why do we insist on educating our future in a manner that allows for many to never reach their full potential? Doing so makes no sense for our society and certainly will never allow for a greater pool of individuals to be trained with necessary skills to make our country a leader in the world once again.

Charter Schools

As a society, we can also no longer allow for the privatization of our public schools. We can no longer allow for charter schools and private schools to pretend they do a better job of meeting the needs of our most in-need students. Society has fallen victim to the belief that the needs of our students are not being met by our public schools. We have been tricked into believing what the media has told us to be the truth: Public schools are using more money and producing less, while charter schools and private schools are getting better results using less money. These lies must not continue. Many Americans, and I have to admit, many teachers I know, believe this to be the gospel truth.

One could argue that charter schools are moderately successful. But I ask you to ponder why charter school students get better grades, do better on standardized tests, and are more successful in college. The simple answer is that these students have parents who care. They have support structures in place that make it easy for them to be successful in ANY school

The Kid in Purple Pants

Structured Approaches to Educating Underprivileged Students

environment. Much as wealthy parents apply for their children to attend a private school, parents who want their students to attend a charter school must also expend energy. They must make a conscious effort to go to the school, fill-out the application, and make an EFFORT to have their child attend this special school. These are the same poor parents who have successful students in my school. Bottom line: They care and want their children to be successful and will do whatever it takes to make it happen.

I remember reading a full-page newspaper ad for the local Catholic high school in my town. The copy bragged that 94% of the students who attended that school went into college upon graduating. I was impressed with the statistics until I realized that each of those families was paying close to $5,000 a year to send their child to that school, and if the students weren't planning on going to college, they would not be attending that school in the first place. These are the parents I have been referring to, those who value education, have had good educational experiences, and have pushed and driven their children to be successful young people.

On more than one occasion I have found myself in impassioned debates over the popular documentary *Waiting for Superman,* which tells the story of how public schools are not meeting the needs of our poor students who come from the inner cities. Millions of people have jumped on the charter school bandwagon and feel it is the best way to educate our students. Actually, charter schools, even with all the loose regulations, application process, and modified expectations, are not faring as well as many first thought. To wit, in one part of the film, parents and students are waiting for the big drawing to occur to find out if a child would be going to the new charter school the following school year. I watched and hoped that these parents, who had worked so hard, were able

The Kid in Purple Pants

Structured Approaches to Educating Underprivileged Students

to get their children into these schools. They understood the importance of a structured environment and how each child thrives when given a chance to be successful. It was heartbreaking to watch as many were denied entry into these schools. However, what saddened me more was the fact that all of these parents wholeheartedly felt that their child was never going to taste success because of their misfortune of not being allowed entry into these schools.

I wanted to stand and scream at the top of my lungs, "The charter school is not the answer to your problems—you are!" Think about it—if all public schools were filled with parents who were not disenfranchised with the school system, and if each child had a parent who believed with all of his or her heart that education and love were the key to happiness, we would have no worries for public education. Unfortunately, this is not the case. Charter schools, in many instances, simply weed out those parents who do not value school. They require a specific amount of service hours, parent meetings, and a host of other responsibilities before they allow a student to attend.

Could you imagine trying to mandate that in a public school? Such demands are unrealistic for many parents, some of whom can't find enough time to check a book bag for homework each evening, let alone volunteer hours toward extracurricular activities at a school. Charter schools are not meeting the needs of those children; rather, they are simply recruiting those students who have a strong support network and a means of succeeding. Why don't charter schools go in search of those parents who dodge phone calls, refuse to attend parent/teacher conferences, send their children to school emotionally drained, and have no resources to make their children's education a pleasant experience? Because if they did, they would be in the exact situation as public schools. It

The Kid in Purple Pants

Structured Approaches to Educating Underprivileged Students

seems that if we are going to use taxpayer money to charter new schools, they should also meet the needs of those children who do not have a safety net at home.

Standardized Testing

Of all the initiatives that adversely affect public education, none has done as much damage as No Child Left Behind (NCLB). The NCLB program has created an environment where high-stakes testing drives the curriculum of every classroom in every school in every district across America. Thanks to the program, schools have been forced to pour resources they do not have into making certain that the strict mandates facing them are met. Is it possible to ever meet these requirements and "beat" the test? No. It is designed so that schools fail. NCLB mandates that all schools meet specific requirements on a yearly basis in order to remain in good standing. State testing, as a result of this law, has become the number one priority in schools throughout the nation. The effects of the law have influenced curriculum, funding procedures, and many other aspects of the everyday functions of a school system. It is important for all to know and understand what this law is actually doing to the education system in America and how it is negatively influencing teachers, administrators, curriculums, and most of all, students.

NCLB requires that all children in grades 3–8 be tested in reading and mathematics and that they must be proficient in both by 2014. The ability of students to perform well on a given test decides a school's assumed success. Specific guidelines and expectations are in place to determine if a school has met Adequate Yearly Progress (AYP). If students are not meeting AYP, schools are placed on watch lists and quickly deemed inadequate if AYP isn't achieved in a specified num-

The Kid in Purple Pants

Structured Approaches to Educating Underprivileged Students

ber of years. Consequently, schools across the nation have been forced to shut down because of low scores on these tests. Charter schools and alternative means of educating students have become the norm in many low-income neighborhoods and communities.

We have begun a new era of extreme item teaching that severely narrows the curriculum. Because of this, students are not being exposed to many useful and crucial aspects of a well-rounded curriculum. I understand the pressure and the need to perform well on the state tests, but a broad curriculum would help students much more than item teaching. Teaching to the test does not enable students the opportunity to develop as critical thinkers and cognitive learners, which is exactly what colleges and universities are looking for in their students.

The injustice being distributed to our students is not the fault of teachers, many of whom do not realize they are hampering students by instructing them on these tests. On the contrary, most teachers feel that they are actually helping by giving students the knowledge they need to do well on the test while making sure that their school meets the state mandates. Not much can be done to change the current trend of teaching the test until pressure is taken off of teachers. And with the ever-increasing percentages needed to reach AYP, teachers are actually devoting more of their time to item teaching.

NCLB has caused a shock wave throughout the public schools of the United States and has created a sense of urgency in teachers that forces them to take drastic measures to indemnify good scores that allow for AYP. Before this legislation was enacted, teachers still wanted their students to perform soundly on state tests but were not under such intense pressure to perform to a specific mandated standard. State tests were a good way to assess if students were actually

The Kid in Purple Pants

Structured Approaches to Educating Underprivileged Students

learning many of the state standards. Teachers and administrators used the tests to help measure where improvements could be made and curriculum development could be enhanced. Its impact on current curriculum trends is drastically influencing teaching methods, materials taught, and time on task. Educators must understand that narrowing the scope of a school's curriculum to better address test material is detrimental to a district's overall ability to educate students into those with knowledge of all subject matter.

As an eighth-grade English and literature teacher, I narrowed my scope and sequence to cover only those specific standards that are tested. When the Illinois Standards Achievement Test (ISAT) no longer assessed writing skills, I stopped focusing on writing and utilized that extra teaching time to review and drill my students on literary devices and only those things that would be on the test. I was not proud of what I was doing. I was very aware of the choice I was making, but the demands I was facing from my administration and the community pressure to maintain AYP for our district were overwhelming. I tried to convince myself that I would be able to do just as good a job of teaching writing skills after the test was over, but deep down I knew that by devoting four more weeks to reviewing for the test, I would never be able to give writing the attention it so deserves.

Regardless of one's politics, the impact of NCLB on curriculum trends in many American schools is enormous to say the least. All would agree that increasing student performance is something teachers and administrators strive for. Because of NCLB, teachers find themselves forced to cut time from other important areas to better envelop test material that will determine if a school meets AYP. It cannot be overstated that NCLB has narrowed the curriculum so much that many students are not being exposed to nearly enough social studies,

The Kid in Purple Pants

Structured Approaches to Educating Underprivileged Students

science, fine arts, and physical education courses that are fundamental in a student's ability to be well-rounded and able to function in society.

Please make no mistake on how I feel about NCLB: The implementation of this program was a deliberate, calculated attempt to end the public education system as we know it. I believe it was a conscious effort to privatize education and discredit the public school systems. There was a campaign to harm the reputation of struggling poor school districts while publicizing the benefits the new mandates had on other districts able to adjust curriculums so that they were able to teach students enough to pass the test. What do I mean? The most underfunded and struggling districts were the first to suffer from NCLB. If they were declared to be underachieving, they were closed, privatized, or converted into charter schools. But, because the law was supposedly created to leave no child behind, the choice of school was at the option of the students. Here's the rub, however: The more affluent schools that were meeting these mandates were not accepting students. For instance, my district would have been an excellent school of choice for those students in East St. Louis whose schools had been deemed unfit. But, did we have to accept them and enable these students to strive forward and achieve? No. Did we get offered additional funding to help these students? Again, no. So, what happened to these students? Many have stayed in the exact same schools because the district was unable to find other schools willing to establish "cooperative agreements" that would allow those students to transfer to a district making AYP. Consequently, the students continue to underperform and the schools receive stricter sanctions and mandates they will never be able to achieve.

Teaching for tests is hopefully a short-lived curriculum for many school districts. The future for school systems

The Kid in Purple Pants

Structured Approaches to Educating Underprivileged Students

seems bleak if changes to the current system are not made. Every school seems doomed to failure under the current system and each student is being prepared for a test and not for becoming educated in all aspects of academia.

In all, we must help open the eyes of people who do not realize that NCLB is forcing school closings in high-poverty communities and slowly spreading to other schools. It may have been ratified in an attempt to help ensure that all students are learning and that all teachers are doing their best to educate our youth, but the program may doom public education.

The Kid in Purple Pants

Structured Approaches to Educating Underprivileged Students

Chapter 8

Leaving Nothing to Chance

"No one cares how much you know,
until they know how much you care."

—Theodore Roosevelt

As I think of the future of public education, I hate to imagine that we will stay stagnant and not see the errors of our ways. For too long we have allowed industrial-age thinking and social stigmas to rule how we meet the needs of our children. I often think of former students who I was not able to "reach," either because of my shortcomings or their upbringing. To my chagrin, I didn't meet their needs and instill in them a drive to do their best in school. I wonder how they would have performed differently if they were offered after-school tutoring and character education that would have taught them how to handle a school environment and deal with frustration and anger. To be sure, my hit-or-miss approach to educating was working for many of my students. I am proud of what I accomplished in the classroom, and I enjoyed every single day I was a teacher. In fact, I miss it so badly sometimes it hurts. But, I don't think I would have ever grown into a well-rounded educator who understands the complex components of how to reach all children if I had stayed a teacher. It truly takes a "systematic approach" (although the approach depends on each school's needs) to at least give all students the opportunity to succeed. Once the approach is in place, only then can

The Kid in Purple Pants

Structured Approaches to Educating Underprivileged Students

it be molded into a game plan for success. When you spot a problem in your classroom, building, or district, tackle that problem with the knowledge that if you are to make a difference, you can't leave it to chance.

I am not advocating for comprehensive school reform models and programs that are sold by developers and huge for-profit companies. I have worked with implementing a CSR model. It did wonders for some components of our district. It was a huge success in helping us streamline our curriculum. We learned the advantages of collaborating, sequencing, and teamwork. At the same time, it didn't give us strategies for making certain our new, wonderful curriculum was being learned by all. It didn't provide us the professional development to deal with learning styles or extremely diverse student populations. In essence, this type of model doesn't offer checks and balances.

Instead, I am proposing that we recognized that each school is unique in its needs. Schools must hone an approach to helping students that is just as distinctive as each student attending the school. Thus a model doesn't account for these subtle nuances in a school population. We must leave nothing to chance. I've repeated this mantra many times throughout this work. All I am asking and advocating for is that we take the loopholes out of education, a course of action that dictates for processes to be established that mandate all children have an equal opportunity at receiving a quality education. Yet, this course of action must comprise a process that accounts for the unique needs of underprivileged students.

What I am trying to achieve is actually quite simple. I want more teachers like Miss Magurany, smiling, encouraging, and caring about a little boy who was so excited about a homophones spelling test in first grade. I want to continue hiring 25-year-old physical education teachers who, in a job

The Kid in Purple Pants

Structured Approaches to Educating Underprivileged Students

interview, say that what they are most proud of is taking guardianship of their little brothers and raising them as their own children (even though they themselves were still children when they did it). I want to witness a veteran teacher cry in my office because she had her "aha" moment during a field trip in which she spotted one of her poor students eating food from a trash can. I only want to hire principals who laugh, cry, and enjoy the struggles of helping a first-grader learn all the necessary tools to be successful in school. I want to continue working with school boards who are not afraid to pioneer new and innovative initiatives that bestow life-changing opportunities to their students.

Am I asking too much? I don't think so. Now is the time to see our most needy students for what they are. Our obligation. Our future. Our greatest asset.

The Kid in Purple Pants

Structured Approaches to Educating Underprivileged Students

If we want to invest in the prosperity
of our nation, we must invest in the
education of our children so that
their talents may be
fully employed.

Bill Clinton

Epilogue

I guess there were a lot of reasons for writing this book, and now that I've come to the end I find it difficult to tell you what has influenced me most in life. Is it my experiences as a successful educator or as an administrator? Was it those instances when I did the right thing and made a difference? Or perhaps it was those times when I knew I did the wrong thing and didn't have the experience, age, or training to make a difference in the students who needed me the most. Was it the initiatives, programs, and grants I had a hand in implementing? Truthfully, I would have to say my family has been my greatest influence.

Although the road to accomplishing what we wanted to do in life was not easy for any of us in the Anderson household, we traveled it together and did our best to do as our parents told us. As I mentioned earlier, my parents stressed that the true measure of one's success was how happy that person was. "Don't allow yourself to **not** do what you want to do." These words were repeated to us over and over, as well as, "Pick your career on what will fulfill you and make you happy. It's the only thing that is going to matter when it's all said and done."

I've followed those words to this day, and I'd venture to say that my parents' sage advice has resonated with all of my siblings. Like me, they were given the same opportunities, encouragement, and taught never to give up no matter how hard the path that lay before them.

My brother Harry epitomizes why we all must strive to meet the needs of our students who come from struggling families. He is one of the most successful professionals I

The Kid in Purple Pants

Structured Approaches to Educating Underprivileged Students

know. His law practice thrives, he is happily married, and he spends plenty of time on vacation. He is also the most loving and caring human being I have ever met. He is the perfect uncle to his nieces and nephews and is the only person I know who has ever given a cat insulin shots because it would, in his words, "enhance its state of existence." As a child he was the protector, the person who watched out for all of us while we were away from home. This was no easy task. As a 12-year-old, he had no clue what he was doing. He just knew that he had been taught to be proud of who he was and to not allow anyone to break his spirit or that of his siblings. Harry could have very well written this book about his experiences, thoughts, doubts, and plenty of fights during his early education. He was the one forced to blaze the trail for the rest of us.

In one of my favorite memories of Harry, I was visiting him at law school during his first year. He lived in one of the worst apartments I have ever seen. He would spend every waking hour studying or working so that he would have enough money to eat. His loans to pay for his education were astronomical, but he never let on that he was worried. But as I look back now, the things he said and did make me realize that he was scared to death of failing. I remember him explaining that the first year of law school is when they try to make you quit. It's where the irresponsible and lazy students are thinned from the herd. Could he have lived with his buddies, shared rent, and lived in a nicer place? Yes. Yet he realized that in order to fulfill his aspirations, he needed to remain focused on the task at hand. Not even the temptation of companionship was enough to make Harry stray from his game plan. He was focused on doing what he set out to accomplish. He knew that all eyes were on him, and four siblings were looking at him and wondering, "Can one of us really do this?"

The Kid in Purple Pants

Structured Approaches to Educating Underprivileged Students

My brother Michael was also our protector. He knew his place in the pecking order and would take orders from Harry on what needed to be done and how he was never to allow anything to happen to us. He worked his way through college, got his first geology job even before he had graduated, and started to help his family. He would allow me to borrow his car, give me money, and keep me on track with my education.

One of my all-time favorite memories of Michael happened on my last day of high school. When he picked me up at school, he congratulated my achievement and then said, "Pat, remember what Paul Simon said, 'When I look back on all the crap I learned in high school, it's a wonder I can think at all.'" He then told me that now was the real time to start figuring out what I wanted to do and that I would have to work hard to accomplish my goals. I had heard it all before from my parents, but as he said it, still in college himself, I knew he was being serious and didn't want to see me fall through the cracks. He was being a big brother.

My sister, Karla, is a whole different story. As I say that, I respect her determination more than that of any other person I know. Karla is smart. Very smart. However, her road to education was sometimes diverted by her love of adventure and quest for happiness. Through persistence, she ultimately got her degree because she knew that it would allow her to provide for her family. The day Karla graduated she said, "You guys didn't really think I wouldn't finish school, did you? I would have never been able to live that down."

Last but not least is my little brother, Kyle. I guess, in a lot of ways, I was to him what Harry was to me. Although birth order deigns him my little brother, he has always been my hero, with his grit, courage, and moral fortitude. Kyle has a real ability to make each person feel special and unique, and I delight in watching him interact with people.

The Kid in Purple Pants

Structured Approaches to Educating Underprivileged Students

My proudest moment as a big brother was the day I watched Kyle speak in front an enormous group of laborers who had come out in droves to support his most recent campaign. As they listened to him speak, I saw that they understood his passion was genuine and that he truly cared about them and their livelihood. As they clapped and cheered, I realized that people respected his desire to do what was right, no matter what the cost. They understood he was just like them. Although he now wears a tie, he is always a roofer at heart.

What each of my siblings represents is what I want for my students. I want them to have the courage, conviction, desire, and ability to do whatever their hearts desire simply because they have been given the opportunity, encouragement, and necessary support to do so. As educators, we do not have the means to change the entire world, but we do have the ability to make our students realize that they can do whatever they want. I want my students to feel as I did as a child—loved, supported, encouraged, and with the ability to know that I could do what I wanted.

I hope no one mistakes my intentions. The road to happiness for my siblings and me happened to be through higher education. This is, by no means, the only way a person can be happy. Happiness is the ONLY real measure of success. We have one life to live and if it is to be a SUCCESSFUL life, it must first be a HAPPY life. Like my mother often said, "All that matters in life is being happy, so give yourself the opportunity to do what you love." If I had loved roofing with all my heart and decided to stay in the business, I know my mother would have been just as proud of me as she was the day I graduated college. Like my mother did for her children, I too encourage my students to do what will make them happy.

The Kid in Purple Pants

Structured Approaches to Educating Underprivileged Students

Biography

Patrick Anderson is the superintendent of Wood River-Hartford School District #15 in Wood River, Illinois. He has worked in schools for nearly 20 years, in the roles of educator, principal, and superintendent. His efforts to provide the best possible education to the students who are most in need have become a passion and an opportunity to share many successes to teachers and administrators in Illinois.

Acknowledgments

Although it would be impossible to thank everyone who has played a part in creating this book, I must thank my family first for their help, encouragement, and support during this process. Although my mother passed away more than 11 years ago, not a day goes by that I don't think about her. I try to remember all of the wisdom she possessed and tried to impress upon me in her short 56 years on earth. She was the master at enjoying life's simple pleasures. Blowing bubbles, a "shower bath" from a garden hose on a hot summer day, fried potatoes and milk gravy on a Sunday morning, and singing to us on the front porch as the sun was setting on fall days were all she needed to be happy. I want to thank my Mom and Dad for showing me that having compassion for others is a virtue, not a weakness. My parents showed all their children that they had worth and were worthy of dignity and respect even if the only pair of pants they owned were purple. But most of all, I want to thank them for encouraging me to share with all my

| The Kid in Purple Pants |

Structured Approaches to Educating Underprivileged Students

students and teachers the need to foster love, compassion, and dignity into every person we have the privilege of influencing.

Also, thank you to all my colleagues in Oakland, Illinois, for their support and help when I was a "rookie" teacher. A special thank you to Steve Amizich, Gina James, Ed Graves, and Cassy Shelton for all their guidance throughout our time together as educators. I want to express my appreciation to Vince Hughes for being such a great friend and support in our pursuit to finish our doctorate programs. Thank you to Brad Keim for designing such a great cover and for being one of the greatest art teachers in the world. My deepest gratitude goes to Jim Burgett for his support and encouragement in making this book a reality. I would like to thank Keri O'Brien for her work in editing this book; I couldn't have done this without her. Thank you to Dr. Alison Reeves for encouraging me to undertake this project and believing that it could actually do some good. I would like to thank the Lavite family, my St. Bernard's classmates, and my former teachers for making my childhood so memorable. And a special thank you to my entire Central School family: You have all made helping children become a quest rather than a job.

The Kid in Purple Pants

Structured Approaches to Educating Underprivileged Students

Index

The Kid in Purple Pants

Structured Approaches to Educating Underprivileged Students

The Kid in Purple Pants

Structured Approaches to Educating Underprivileged Students

The Kid in Purple Pants

Structured Approaches to Educating Underprivileged Students

The Kid in Purple Pants

Structured Approaches to Educating Underprivileged Students

The Kid in Purple Pants

Structured Approaches to Educating Underprivileged Students

The Kid in Purple Pants

Structured Approaches to Educating Underprivileged Students

The Kid in Purple Pants

Structured Approaches to Educating Underprivileged Students

The Kid in Purple Pants

Structured Approaches to Educating Underprivileged Students

The Buck Stops With Us!

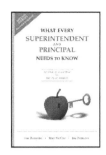

Jim Rosborg, Max McGee, and Jim Burgett

Contents: School Leadership, Civic Leadership and Ethics; Business Basics for School Leaders; Communications; Building and Sustaining Trust; Planning; Expert Knowledge; Building Internal Capacity; Visionary Leadership; Successful Teaching and Learning; Adventures in Innovation; Taking Care of You; Standards, Assessment, and Accountability, and Case Studies in Real World Leadership.

ISBN 0910167214 / Trade Paperback, $24.95, Digital, $20
2nd ed., 2008 / www.superintendents-and-principals.com

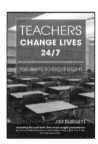

Teachers Change Lives 24/7

Jim Burgett

Read the testimonials, a sample chapter, and Jim's credentials at the website above and you'll see why the stories, passion, and fun he has shared on the lecture circuit for a decade has principals and superintendents buying the book by the boxload to help inject purpose, pride, and zest into their schools and districts.

ISBN 0910167915 / Trade Paperback, $17.95, Digital, $14
2007 / www.teacherschangelives.com

Education Communication Unlimited
(800) 563-1454 / P.O. Box 845, Novato, CA 94947

The
Perfect
School

Jim Rosborg, Max McGee, and Jim Burgett

How can one talk about achieving or even approaching perfection in schools without a definition, a roadmap, and a sense of the features and steps required to get there? Here, the three top award-winning leaders who wrote *What Every Superintendent and Principal Needs to Know* combine their skills, again, to look at perfect teachers, perfect staff, perfect parents, perfect principals (plus 10 more chapters), to start the quest.

ISBN 9780910167901 / Trade Paperback, $24.95, Digital, $20
2007 / www.superintendents-and-principals.com

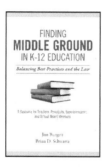

Finding
Middle
Ground

Jim Burgett and Brian D. Schwartz

Brian Schwartz masterfully makes complex laws understandable while Jim Burgett magically creates win-win situations. Here, the two prize-winning educators balance best practices and the law in a compelling book that's full of practicality, reality, humor, and common sense. "It should be required reading by every educator everywhere" is what we hear most.

ISBN 9780979629563 / Trade Paperback, $24.95, Digital, $20
2009 / www.middlegroundforeducators.com

Education Communication Unlimited
(800) 563-1454 / P.O. Box 845, Novato, CA 94947